Dragons in My Classroom

Dragons in My Classroom

A Teacher's Memoir

Barbara Kennard

SHE WRITES PRESS

Published 2022
Printed in the United States of America
Print ISBN: 978-1-64742-365-0
E-ISBN: 978-1-64742-366-7
Library of Congress Control Number: 2021924251

For information, address:
She Writes Press
1569 Solano Ave #546
Berkeley, CA 94707

She Writes Press is a division of SparkPoint Studio, LLC.

All company and/or product names may be trade names, logos, trademarks, and/or registered trademarks and are the property of their respective owners.

Names and identifying characteristics have been changed to protect the privacy of certain individuals.

For KBM

Love is not love which alters when it alternation finds,

Or bends with the remover to remove.

O no, it is an ever fixed mark

That looks on tempests and is never shaken;

It is the star to every wand'ring bark. . . .

—William Shakespeare, Sonnet 116

For every day . . . those who were doing us some good
. . . knew it was never enough but hoped to improve
a little by living.

    —W. H. Auden, "In Memory of Sigmund Freud"

And thou shalt see how apt it is to learn. Any hard
lesson . . . may do thee good.

    —William Shakespeare, *Much Ado About Nothing*

If I take the wings of the morning
and dwell in the uttermost parts of the sea,
Even there your hand will lead me
and your right hand hold me fast.

                        —Psalm 139:8–9

Contents

Introduction. 1

Chapter 1: A Blessing in Disguise. 7

Chapter 2: *Arduus ad Solem* 27

Chapter 3: Glimpsing God. 47

Chapter 4: Lost and Found 63

Chapter 5: Tough Love. 85

Chapter 6: A Dragon Teacher Now. 95

Chapter 7: Difficult Choices. 112

Chapter 8: The Beginning of the End. 125

Chapter 9: Back in the USA. 147

Chapter 10: Unexpected Gifts 171

Chapter 11: New Millennium, New Job. 185

Chapter 12: And All Shall Be Well 202

Epilogue 208

Acknowledgments. 220

About the Author 223

Introduction

I knew I wanted to be a teacher in 1959, when I was six years old. Miss Gluding, my first-grade teacher, was kind and firm. There was no dilly-dallying around with her. She instilled in me a small, healthy sense of fear and a large dose of compassion. Today, we cringe at the idea of a teacher making students feel a little fearful, but it actually helped me learn. I knew from her eagle eye that she meant business when I fooled around in class, but I also felt her compassion for me when I struggled to read. I can still see her sitting next to me in the hallway outside her classroom, our chairs side by side, her small, gray-haired head bent over, watching and listening to me with all her attention, as I read aloud from *Our New Friends*, one of the many titles in the Dick and Jane series.

I read fast and with mistakes. But Miss Gluding said gently, with a twinkle in her other eye, "Oops, Barbara, one whole line skipped right out off the page. Where did it go? Let's try again with this index card. When you keep your place, you read very well."

My mistakes frustrated me, and the fact that I was born almost completely blind in my right eye was no excuse, as far as I was concerned. I worked at something until I got it right. I reasoned, *I may not have much vision in my right eye, but I will strive to be perfect in other ways.*

Miss Gluding was a saint with me. When I grew impatient with myself, she smiled and encouraged me not to give up. She never asked me to "get it all right"; she offered me strategies and asked me to try again. I wanted to be a teacher, like Miss Gluding.

I started very early on my journey toward perfection and never gave up trying to compensate for my poor eyesight and dyslexia, which no one knew anything about, let alone the word itself, when I was in school. Other teachers, who didn't have Miss Gluding's empathy, embarrassed me by calling attention to my mistakes. I remember the terrible humiliation I felt from my sixth-grade teacher's words when I couldn't spell correctly. "Barbara," Miss Bell announced for the whole class to hear, "You have not spelled *fascination* correctly. Once again, you have reversed the *c* and the *s*. You will not be able to read and write very well next year in seventh grade if you cannot spell correctly. Copy it twenty-five times at recess."

I wiped my eyes. I loved to read and write and couldn't wait to be in seventh grade. I copied *fascination* twenty-five times in my best Palmer cursive.

Whenever Miss Bell made me feel bad about my spelling, I tried to recall kind and strong Miss Gluding, and what she had written on my report card: "Barbara is a very good reader." But because of my painful sixth-grade year, I decided instead that when I became a teacher, I wouldn't yell at a kid for misspelling a word like *fascination*, or make her stay in from recess to copy it twenty-five times. I would be a better teacher than Miss Bell.

Yet, in striving to be a better teacher than she, I actually became more like her. At least I knew better than to speak to my students the way Miss Bell spoke to me, for the most part. Instead, I substituted her language for unattainable expectations of myself and my students. By the time I started teaching, in 1980, I was so far down the road to perfection that I honestly thought my expectations weren't all that stringent. I reasoned that even the kindest and best of my teachers had demanded a great deal from me, and I carried this standard right into my own teaching.

From 1983 to 1987, I taught fifth and sixth grades at a Montessori school in Pasadena, California. My students were classic Montessori kids: quirky, wise beyond their years, capable of the unusual. They thrived on challenge and were themselves somewhat inclined toward the sublime. I was in my element these four years. My own Montessori teacher, Madame Kripulani, who had learned from Maria Montessori herself, passed on the rigors of her training to her students. First and foremost, we were taught that of all the different versions of Montessori education, the Association Montessori Internationale (AMI) possessed the purest curriculum and philosophy about the education of young children. An AMI classroom was not child-centered in the way we think of this concept in the twenty-first century; children did not have free rein with classroom materials. Though they were unique and enticing, there were particular ways in which to use them, which were just as sacrosanct as their attractiveness. However, once a child demonstrated expertise with a set of materials, she was allowed to explore new uses for them: The geometric shapes became pieces of machinery; graded color tablets evolved into modern-art canvases.

My Montessori students got to know me well, and I them, since we had each other for two years, and of course I had to make the second year, when they were all in sixth grade, even more demanding than fifth grade. I plunged them into harder work, rationalizing that my charges were a year older and a year smarter and needed more challenges. Their faces were incredulous when I asked them to memorize the etymologies of their vocabulary words. My students, eccentric though they were, did not enjoy making endless charts of word origins, as I had in my seventh-grade English class, but they did it probably out of allegiance to and some kind of fear of me. I could be a bit of a dragon, just like Miss Bell, though at the time I had no awareness that I was carrying out my plan from my own sixth-grade experience to be a better teacher than she was.

Soon the school director reminded me of a Montessori hallmark: "At this age, the students must be given the freedom and the time to discover what interests them. If they become curious about word origins, then it will be appropriate for you to point them in the right direction."

Her words sounded out of sync with my AMI training, but I was teaching in an American Montessori Society school, where the curriculum and expectations tend to be more focused on each individual child's abilities and needs. I adjusted my vocabulary lessons by giving students a bit of information about etymology, and, to my delight, a few of them got excited about the origins of some of their favorite spelling words.

While teaching at the Montessori school, I'd also begun to recognize my own learning issues in some of my students' reversed letters and numbers, skipped steps in directions, and mispronounced non-phonetic words. So I decided during my master's work to move into the special-ed field. In 1988, I completed two master's degrees, one in special education, the other in clinical child development. For six years, I taught students with language-related learning disabilities in public schools, which, oddly enough, welcomed my demanding expectations. Special-ed students knew they had to work harder than kids who didn't struggle with dyslexia or dysgraphia. So, for a while, I was again in my element; this time, I could be fairly demanding. And I knew the kind of support my special-needs students required, for, like Miss Gluding, I treated my students with compassion and held them to high expectations. I knew what it was like to struggle and to have unsympathetic teachers. But I also understood how hard kids with learning disabilities would have to work, not just for a period of time, but for their entire lives.

Though successful as a special-ed teacher, after six years, I began to feel the burnout that begins earlier than many teachers in this field realize. It sneaks up on you. I wanted to return to the general classroom and began teaching sixth grade at the Fessenden School, an all-boys school, in the fall of 1993. My early years at Fessy were both rewarding and hard. The former because I taught my passions: classic literature, a bit of Shakespeare, interpretative writing, and grammar. The Junior Great Books series, *Tom Sawyer*, and *The Red Pony* were hits with the boys year after year, although they enjoyed diagramming sentences much more when I created "grammar teams" to play "transitive football."

The hard part about teaching at Fessenden was what had been hard all along. Despite the occasional fun times in class, I was deemed too strict and too demanding by some students, parents, administrators, and other teachers. After four years of struggling with these issues yet again, I began to wonder if teaching was my calling after all. Yet something in me recoiled at the idea of leaving the classroom. I'd loved school all my life, despite the challenges and hard times I'd had as a student and a teacher. I couldn't leave. Leaving would be a kind of dying: I'd feel incomplete, empty as a person. I wanted to spend my life teaching, but I also wanted to be a different teacher, someone who didn't need to be perfect or expect her students to be. To do that, I'd have to shed the "get it all right" persona I'd carried with me since

I was a kid. How to accomplish this feat was unclear to me at first; I just knew with every fiber of my being that I wanted to be a better teacher. Little did I know that a unique opportunity would present itself in the seventeenth year of my career.

Chapter 1
A Blessing in Disguise

I'm in my seventeenth year of teaching English, my fourth at the Fessenden School, a boys' K–9 independent school in the western suburbs of Boston. It's January 1997 at seven thirty on a gray Friday morning. At my desk, writing up lesson plans for the coming week, I sense someone in the doorway and look up to see my department head, Sheila Green. A short, stout woman in her forties, she wears a dark suit with a colorful blouse peeking out of the top of her buttoned-up jacket.

Carrying a pile of books and already looking tired at this hour, Sheila strolls up to my desk and says, "Barbara, I'm glad you're here before the boys arrive. I had several calls yesterday from parents about the test you gave on Monday. Apparently, you asked the students to use all twenty vocabulary words from their weekly lesson in sentences about the books they're reading. What were your goals and objectives for this lesson?"

I pause for a moment to swallow my frustration. I'm forty-four years old. I have seventeen years of experience in the classroom. Yet Sheila's question makes me feel as if I were a beginner. "I'll explain," I offer, raising my left eyebrow ever so slightly. "My intention was to assess the boys' understanding of the definitions and parts of speech of the weekly vocabulary words."

Sheila shifts the books in her arms and retorts, "That seems like a lot to ask of sixth graders in one class period. Some of the boys were stressed by this expectation."

As I walk around to the front of my desk, I hope my thoughts are not obvious to Sheila: *Again? I've tried to adjust my teaching, but kids and parents are still complaining. I have years of experience under my belt; why does Fessenden question my standards?*

I put my hands in the pockets of my skirt and look at Sheila. "I thought it was reasonable, given the boys have been working daily with these words for a week. They made flashcards and practiced them in class. We also read and discussed the passage in their vocabulary books that uses all the words. And they answered questions about it, using the words. The boys were proficient in their work, so I felt they were ready to do something new."

Sheila regards me coolly and shifts the books in her hands again. Enunciating each word, she says, "As I said, that seems like a lot for one class period. Did you consider giving it as a take-home test? Or you could have split up some of the assessment, assigning them half to do one day and the other half, the next. I think they would have found it more manageable if you had chosen one of these strategies."

I hitch a hip on my desk and remind myself that the test is designed to be doable in one class period. And, given the parental intervention I suspect on some of the boys' homework, how will I know for certain if the results on a take-home test won't reflect that involvement? But it doesn't feel safe to voice this directly to Sheila. Talking about parental participation is sort of a no-go area at Fessenden. There's a feeling among faculty that it happens, but since we can't really prove it, it's not worth the possible retribution if we say something we can't support.

Sheila's eyes zero in on me as she continues, "I think your students would feel less pressure if they knew how they're going to be tested."

With that, she puts her books down on a student desk with just the right amount of *thump* to make her point.

"That may be true, but under those circumstances, a test isn't really a test. I want to see how students apply what they know in situations they don't know." I look toward my door as some boys begin to chatter at their cubbies in the hallway.

Sheila follows my gaze and then turns back to me with a smile. "Well, yes, I agree, but you expect too much of your students and, if you don't mind my saying so, too much of yourself."

This sounds familiar. Last fall, Sheila told me my summer reading assignment, to have the boys read three books and write about them in September, was too demanding. I feel so confused about what she wants. On the one hand, I'm too tough, but according to previous moments with Sheila I'm also passionate, well organized, and very knowledgeable about English. I don't know how to change my expectations, and I'm not sure I want to.

I feel Sheila's eyes on me as she continues, "Teaching is a very strenuous job, and if you want to stay in it for the long haul, I encourage you to cut your students and yourself some slack."

Putting on my game face, I enthuse, "Sheila, I appreciate your concern for me. But I think I'd be sending a mixed message to kids if I didn't correct work they know is significant. It seems kind of disrespectful to give them challenging assignments and not assess their effort. The work's hard, but we're having more fun. As you suggested last fall when we discussed my goals for the year, I've made a conscious effort to include some games in our classwork. The boys love the grammar relay race we play."

The hallway noise increases. It's time for first period, and, although I don't have a class, I don't want to spend my free period talking to Sheila. I glance at my door.

She takes my hint, picks up her books, and says, "I've got a class this period, but I'm happy to hear about your grammar game, Barbara. I will make a note of this in your file. And I'll let the parents know the gist of our conversation."

Sheila leaves the room without waiting for a response from me. It's probably a good thing she leaves when she does, since I might've said something I'd regret had she stayed around. I can hear myself now: *Isn't what goes on in the classroom a better way to assess a teacher than what's in her personnel file?* Or, *Why do you come see me only when a parent complains?*

I close the door and sink into one of the reading chairs in the back of the room to ponder my situation. Fessenden wants teachers to challenge kids. Everyone says it's good for kids to work hard. But then when something *is* hard, the school seems to give in to parents by asking the teacher to lighten up. On the other hand, Sheila just said she's happy about my grammar games. Yet she implied that I want things to be perfect, which is probably true. That's just who I am. Besides, sometimes my quest for best helps me tackle new challenges: directing and producing Shakespeare plays; inventing new curricula; staying up to date on new teaching practices. What's wrong with that? I wonder what Sheila's going to tell the parents who called her. Why didn't they talk to me directly? She also said I needed to cut myself some slack. What does she mean? Am I going to be fired if I don't lighten up a bit? I wonder if I should look around just to see what other teaching positions are out there before I have to.

The idea of a job search takes on bigger proportions the following weekend when I see an advertisement in the Sunday *Boston Globe* for a middle-school English teacher position at the Winsor School in Boston. One of the most intellectually challenging and elite girls' schools in New England, Winsor is a significant step up academically from most other independent schools. Surely my standards would fit better there, where expecting a lot from students and teachers is the norm.

I apply for the position and have an initial interview. A week later, I return as a finalist to teach a class in front of the search committee. Members of the committee are highly complimentary, and the headmistress tells me that she anticipates hiring me. But six weeks pass without any word from the school. Finally, in late May, I receive a phone call from the head of the search committee, informing me that Winsor has offered the position to someone who's the "right fit" for the school.

As I listen to her statement, my stomach turns upside down. The English department head told me my lessons were appropriately challenging but fun and interesting, Conversations with the search committee at lunch were so warm and welcoming, I felt as if I were one of them already.

A few days later, I turn in my contract for the 1998–'99 school year to Fred Post, Fessenden's headmaster, an older gentleman with an ever-present twinkle in his eye. He reminds me of Andy Griffiths as he remarks, "I'm sorry the Winsor job didn't work out for you, Barbara, but I'm very glad you'll be back with us next year."

A few days later, as I'm walking to my classroom, John Donovan, Fessenden's assistant head, calls out to me, "Hey, Barbara, can you wait up?" He waves to me as he crosses the small, tree-lined quad between my classroom building and the administration offices. Even though he wears the school's quintessential khaki trousers, blue blazer, and nondescript tie, John stands out with his curly red hair as he bounces like a small bear toward me.

"Hi, John!" I wait for him to reach me, and we shake hands. John has been at Fessenden a long time; as an alum, a parent, a teacher, and now an administrator, he's seen it all and has a unique ability to recognize the school's flaws and strengths from a fairly unbiased perspective. And I taught both his sons in my first three years here, so I've always felt comfortable speaking candidly and confidentially with him. I even told him about my Winsor interview, though it was technically a conflict of interest for us both.

A bit out of breath, John gestures to some nearby benches. We sit across from each other on this breezy May day in the shade of old oak trees. John loosens his tie, leans forward, and says in his soft voice, "Barbara, I spoke with Fred Post the other day about our faculty needs for the fall, and he told me you'll be returning. I'm guessing the Winsor job didn't pan out?"

I nod my head and lean into the back of the bench. "That's right. In a nutshell, I wasn't the 'right fit' for the school, though they didn't tell me why."

John gives me a sympathetic look. "You felt quite optimistic about that job, so it must have been a shock not to get it. We're glad not to lose you, but something obviously isn't working for you here, or you wouldn't be looking for another job."

"Well, yes, you're right, John."

"Would you be willing to tell me confidentially what is difficult for you?"

I brush my hair off my face. "I appreciate your concern and your confidentiality. After four years here, I'm still struggling to find the right tone to my teaching."

John smiles gently; perhaps he recalls some of the complaints he heard about me in 1993, my first year at Fessenden: *She tries to do too much; the boys are still so young; they don't need to be pushed so hard,* but his steady support helped me through that year. I can still hear his words: *The boys need high expectations, but perhaps softening your tone with more "we" statements would help the boys feel as if you're with them.*

Some birds squawk overhead, and we both watch them glide across the pale spring sky. I shift in my seat and add, "I've made some changes, but four years on, parents and administrators still believe I ask too much of the boys. I'm not used to parents playing such a big role in their children's education. When I taught in special-ed and Montessori schools, most parents deferred to a teacher's decision. They expected the work to be challenging."

"And it feels different here?" John asks, cocking his head to one side.

I take a deep breath and glance at the sky. Then I look back at John, see his warm smile, and venture forth. "I feel confused when I'm told my high standards are valued but am simultaneously asked to ease up on them."

John twiddles his tie and reminds me of my recent success. "Last year's sixth-grade Shakespeare play was worlds better than the previous years' because you let the boys do more. So I'm wondering, are there other reasons you want to leave Fessenden?"

No administrator I've ever known has been so empathic: sympathizing with me over the loss of the Winsor job, recognizing that Fessenden feels different from other schools where I've taught. So I explain how my extra, nonteaching duties, for which I am not compensated, give me less time to address the professional goals Fessenden expects of all teachers—to reflect on why I am a teacher, what I'm doing well, and how I can improve my practice.

I can tell from John's smile that he understands my concerns. He stretches his legs and conveys something most administrators would avoid: "Barbara, I appreciate your trust in me to speak so candidly. You're right, we should be paying teachers for their extra duties!" He grins at my raised eyebrows and confides that the school is developing a different salary scale based on points teachers accrue for additional responsibilities. He also explains something I haven't considered: Asking teachers to take on extra work is part and parcel of independent schools, and I would have found this to be true even at Winsor. However, he cheers me when he adds, "I know from observing you in the classroom that teaching is your vocation; you love it, and I can't see you doing anything else. But I also hear that you think a change is needed. Actually, all teachers need a change if we're to stay in this crazy work."

I smile, rest my hand on the bench, and rub the warm wood. Then I whisper, "You're right, I do need a change. I don't know what that might look like for me. I just know that I seem to be at odds with what Fessenden wants from its teachers."

A sheepish smile slips across John's face. "I can relate to your situation. I had some challenges when I arrived here in 1975!" Laughing and slapping his knees, John describes how he created "bogus lesson plans" and allowed "total chaos" in his classroom when he arrived at Fessenden fresh out of college. "Luckily, I had an experience that helped me become a better teacher. I learned about the exchange program Fessenden had with a school in Oxford, England, and in 1978 I swapped jobs with Robin Young, who at that time taught history at the Dragon School. Now he's the headmaster."

John goes on to describe the challenges of learning a very different teaching style at the Dragon School: a different curriculum, different communication with parents, different ways of assessing kids. Eyes twinkling, he tells me, "Nothing about teaching overseas was the same as teaching in the States! It was as if I were starting from scratch, but I did it. I think it could be the same for you. Rather than look for another job in Boston, consider teaching at the Dragon for a year. Then come back to us and see how you feel about being here. Think it over, and let me know if you'd like to be in touch with Robin."

My heart races; grabbing the arm of the bench, I say, "John! Teaching in another country is a wonderful idea. I don't think I would have considered such a thing on my own, but the way you put it and the experience you had excites me. You've been so kind to listen to me and to make this suggestion. I'm very grateful and will let you know whatever I decide."

"I'm glad you're interested," John says as he stands up. "I hope to hear from you soon."

"You will! And thanks again." I offer my hand, and he gives me his.

After John bounds back down the path to his office building, I sit on the bench again to consider all that has just transpired. God works in all our lives in mysterious ways. Losing the Winsor job is not a coincidence; it's a blessing in disguise.

At home that evening, my husband, Brady, and I prepare our favorite soup, *ribollita*, for supper. Brady is a concert pianist and professor of music at Eastern Nazarene College in Quincy, Massachusetts, where we've lived since 1990, when we were married. Since the beginning of our marriage, we have sought each other's insight and support whenever one of us has had a significant opportunity, such as teaching in another country or performing at the White House. These conversations always take place when we're doing something intentional together: preparing a meal, drinking a cup of coffee, or reading.

As we chop veggies in the kitchen, I tell Brady about my conversation earlier that day with John, and we discuss how it might work for us to be in England for a year.

"Barb, this is a gift; you're going to be in Oxford in July for a poetry class at Merton College anyway, and I'll be teaching piano master classes in London. You could write to the head of Dragon and ask to meet with him," Brady says.

"Yes, but, more to the point, how will we do this together next year?" I ask.

Cutting carrots and onions, Brady tells me he could request a sabbatical, but he'll need time to develop and present his plans to the college. Slowly, he adds, "It's too late to accomplish all this for next year, but I could probably take one in the 1998–'99 school year."

Brady looks away. I haven't considered the time limits he's just described. We take a break. I rummage in the fridge for celery. Brady goes to the pantry and returns with some chicken broth. We chop and cook in calm silence for a bit; then he says, "Barb, living overseas for a year is a significant change for us both. Let's not be in a hurry. If it's meant to be, it'll happen in its own good time."

Glaring at Brady, I chop celery into smaller and smaller pieces and tell myself this opportunity doesn't feel as urgent to him as it does to me. Yet I know he's right. As we scrape our veggie bits into the pot of broth, I say, "I wasn't the 'right fit' for Winsor, and I don't seem to 'fit' at Fessenden. I need a change, and sooner would be better than later."

Brady puts down his knife and takes my hand. "You're selling yourself short by saying you don't fit there. You've added something new to your Shakespeare productions. The school values that, so you must fit in some ways." Then he arches his eyebrows to remind me that I've missed something.

For a few more minutes, we focus on soup. I drain and rinse two cans of cannellini beans and dump them in the pot. Brady rummages in the fridge for more leftovers to add to our *ribollita*.

As we finish cooking, Brady asks how going to England to teach will help me feel more comfortable at Fessenden. I take a seat at the small island in the middle of our kitchen and pour us each a glass of wine. He joins me with a bowl of chips. Feeling teary, I sip my wine and remind Brady of all the times parents, administrators, and even he suggested that I'm too much of a perfectionist. Then I admit something I've never really given voice to: "I am too demanding as a teacher. But I don't know how to ease up on myself or my students. Teaching overseas might help me figure that out."

"That's an admirable goal, Barbara, but just how do you think teaching overseas will help you do this?" Brady wonders. I remind him of what John shared with me: that I'll be teaching material I know nothing about, and I'll have to teach differently from the way I teach here. Then I add, "But what really gives me hope is that I'd be unknown at the Dragon."

I continue to share how my tendency to be a perfectionist has been a part of me since I was a child. Whenever something was hard, my dad wanted me to try harder. I can still hear his words: *Barbara, try again. Keep trying until you get it all right.* Dad never asked me to be impeccable, but something in me turned his words into the idea that to be good at something, I had to be superb at it. I watched how hard he worked to give our family a good life. For thirty years or more, he made it possible for us to live in a desirable part of our middle-class town. My brother and I attended private schools, and we always had summer vacations.

Brady smiles knowingly about my father's type-A personality and then asks about my experience in school. I explain that I had some empathetic teachers who knew it was hard for me and supported me. They didn't ask me to "get it all right." Instead, they emphasized strong effort and perseverance. I also share something more difficult and describe how other teachers' harsh words made me feel poorly about myself. *Barbara, you failed this math class last year; you may fail again if you don't work harder.*

With sweet understanding, Brady says, "I see now why this exchange could be a life-changing experience for you."

"I hope so. I've been trying to prove to myself and my teachers, long after I passed through their classes, that not only was I a good student, I was perfect."

Brady picks up my train of thought. "As if to say, *See, you were wrong!*"

I nod in agreement. "I equate working hard with excellence and now impose this expectation on myself as a teacher and my students. I don't want to do that, but I don't know how to do things differently, so I hope that teaching in England will show me how to be more patient and less demanding of myself and others, not just in the classroom, but in life. Cultivating English friends and traveling to places associated with the literature I love will help too."

"You have strong insight about yourself, Barb! I'm proud of you."

"Thanks, lovey. I'm a bit of a slow learner, but when I get it, I get it!"

Laying out my school clothes later that night, I ponder all this in the quiet beating of my heart. I'm taking a new road, one I've not yet traveled, but with God's help I hope to become the teacher I'm meant to be. I haven't talked much about my sense of perfect self, perhaps out of fear that I'd be judged or that someone will actually agree with me. Yet I hear Eleanor Roosevelt's words in my head: *No one can make you feel inferior without your consent.* I determine in this moment that I will not continue to let the language of past teachers, or even my beloved father's words, make me feel as if I have to be faultless in order to be good. My best effort, however flawed it may be, will be enough.

It's mid-July 1997, and I've been in Oxford for the first week of the two-week poetry class I was scheduled to take months before John Donovan and I discussed the Dragon School possibility. Today, a rather hot Saturday for England, I walk a mile or more from my rooms at Merton College, one of the twenty-four colleges of Oxford University, to Gee's Restaurant to meet with Robin Young, the Dragon School headmaster. As I make my way up the Banbury Road, Oxford's main drag, I pass bed-and-breakfasts and academic buildings constructed from the famous golden Cotswold stone. Box-shaped buses and little lorries dodge cyclists on the road. Trees abundantly line both sides of the road, and gardens exist everywhere, even in tiny plots by the bus stops. Approaching the restaurant, I see Robin, a tall, slim man with graying temples, wearing tan linen trousers and a white polo shirt. He's standing next to his bicycle. He puts down his bike helmet and strides toward me. Although this is our first meeting, somehow he recognizes me. I guess I don't look English.

Robin steps up and extends his hand. "Barbara Kennard?"

"Yes! And you must be Robin Young?" We shake hands.

"Indeed! I am delighted to meet you. You must have walked here from the college. Let's get inside," Robin says, as he escorts me to the restaurant and opens the door for me.

Inside the restaurant's glass conservatory, Robin confirms the reservation he made for a noon seating and the hostess shows us to a table set with white linens and china. Green plants of all kinds surround the small dining space. A ceiling fan provides some relief from the heat. After we order our meals, Robin gets right to the point.

"Barbara, I am so pleased John inspired you to contact me. I remember him and my time at Fessy with much delight. We've not done an exchange between the two schools since, so I am glad you've resurrected it. I can't offer you any campus housing, but I will suss out a reasonably priced flat for you to rent in Oxford, hopefully not too far from the school. And I also must tell you that we can't possibly do the exchange until the 1998–'99 school year. Do these stipulations put you off, or may we continue to plan for it?"

I smile and reply, "We can certainly plan for the exchange in 1998–'99. Brady, my husband, most likely cannot take his sabbatical until that year anyway, and we'd be happy to rent a flat in Oxford."

Robin raises his water glass and says, "Cheers! Then that's settled! Now, tell me a bit about what you hope for from this experience."

Oh! I wasn't expecting to be asked this. But, of course, it makes sense. Surely, he can't just take my word or John's recommendation for doing an exchange, especially since it's been out of use for years.

A server arrives with our grapefruit-and-avocado starters. I put my napkin in my lap and answer Robin's question. "After sixteen years in the business, I feel the need to reinvent myself, to shed a few bad habits and learn new ways to teach. I'm not sure what that would look like here, but based on what John shared about his experience, I imagine it would involve teaching a different curriculum and adapting to the English educational system. Since I'd be here for only one year, I'd like to teach a variety of grades. In most of the schools where I've taught, it hasn't been possible to move out of a particular grade level. I've been teaching fifth and sixth grades for ten years and would welcome the chance to teach older and younger children."

After telling Robin I want to shed some "bad habits," I worry if he'll ask me to elaborate, but he doesn't, and I'm not about to go on about my perfectionism.

Swallowing some of his salad, Robin replies, "You are quite right to learn as much as you can about our system. The best way to do that would be to teach 'across the school,' which many of our teachers do. We don't group students into 'grades,' as you do in the States; we group them by age, and our student body is composed of boys and girls ages nine to thirteen. Now, what else can I tell you?"

I like Robin's direct but respectful tone. I can tell by this point in our conversation that he's easy to talk to. "I'm curious about how teachers and parents work together at the Dragon," I say. Hearing bits of other diners' conversations, I am reminded that English people can be quite discreet when discussing business matters in public, and I wonder, *Is my question too direct? It would be at Fessenden, but I'm not at Fessenden, and Robin has asked me in all sincerity to tell him what I hope to experience here.*

Robin looks directly at me and explains, "Form takers—at Fessenden you call them advisors—have age-level meetings twice a year in the evenings with parents. You'll have fifteen students in your form, and each parent meeting lasts about twenty minutes." Robin also explains how teachers gather student information from colleagues during designated meeting times. I won't have to collect this material from colleagues on my own time, as I would at Fessenden, between classes, in the hallways, or on the phone at night.

More diners arrive for lunch, and the noise level increases to just below bedlam, so Robin scooches his chair closer to mine. Then he stresses another important point: "Dragon parents leave matters to the school. They understand it's our job to discipline pupils and expect all of us to have very high standards for good behavior and strong effort. A Dragon teacher addresses problematic children on the spot and gets on with teaching the class."

How different from Fessenden! It would be considered an invasion of a boy's privacy and could cause him to feel humiliated if a teacher spoke to him about his behavior in front of his peers.

Our server returns with our entrées, and we pause while he places them in front of us.

"Robin, you are most gracious. All this sounds wonderful. So much of what you describe is what I hope for with this exchange. I'm very excited. Thank you," I say, and take a bite of my chicken-salad croissant.

Robin gestures to a server for more water and remarks, "I'm pleased too. 'Twill be good fun to have a Fessy teacher here after all these years since my exchange with John."

Returning to Fessenden in the fall of 1997, I present the idea of an exchange between the two schools to Fred Post, our headmaster, who says, "Barbara, I'm so pleased! This will be a wonderful experience for you, and by doing this exchange, you're creating opportunities for your colleagues to do the same in the future." He contacts Robin and makes the arrangement official. In September 1998, Dragon teacher Jim Cameron will come to Fessenden to teach my classes, and I will go to the Dragon to teach his. Once we've confirmed the arrangement, Brady applies for and is granted his sabbatical. But there's a hitch. He has too many varied responsibilities in the music department for one person to be able to fulfill them for a whole year. The faculty dean offers Brady a half-year sabbatical, from December 1998 to June 1999.

We discuss Brady's offer when he comes home on a snowy January day in 1998 with this news. While he practices some Bach, I make hot chocolate and wish he'd play some jazz or something from a Broadway musical. Sure, we've been apart when he's gone on concert tours, but those separations were for only two to three weeks, and I stayed here in my own home, in my own country. How will I cope by myself in a foreign land for four months? Well, for starters, I tell myself, I'm going to remember the trip I took to England by myself in 1988, after getting my master's degree. Ten years on, I think I'll still be able to draw on that experience.

The next day, Brady comes in the back door and shakes snow off. After I help him remove all the accoutrements of winter, I slump into the chair in our back hallway. He tries to cheer me up: "Barb, this isn't what we hoped for, but it's what we have. Besides, we each have a history of being on our own. When we married, you were thirty-seven, I forty-three. We'd each lived alone for many years. We can do this again for four months. We'll be okay."

Brady always sees the glass as half full. I could grouse about it, I could let my fears of going alone stop me, but I want this exchange so much that for once in my life I take his cue and do the same. This is how it has to be.

Soaking in my nightly bath, I muse about my fortunes. My school has created this exchange. My husband supports me 100 percent. And I have goals that I hope and pray will make me a better teacher and enrich my life beyond what I can envision right now. Indeed, the creator of the universe gives us far more than we can ask for or imagine.

Brady and I use nicknames, usually to tease each other, to make a point, or to show tenderness. We made these up not long after we became engaged, in 1989. I started it by calling him Bear, and he soon came up with Bearess, his idea of a kind of feminization of Bear.

"Bearess, you've been packing and repacking two suitcases for weeks! Your flight to Gatwick leaves in three hours; we should leave for the airport before you decide to unpack them again!" Brady calls to me from the front hall of our home in Quincy on the last day of August 1998.

"I'm coming, Bear! Just closing my suitcases!"

Down in the front hall, I take a long look around this wonderful house the two of us have called home since 1990. So many gatherings we have had here: dinner parties, holiday celebrations, neighborhood meetings, house concerts with Brady's musician friends. I look out the window at our beloved garden and across the road to Quincy Bay and the playground by the beach. Here, all of Victoria Road gathers for picnics in the summer and decoration of the neighborhood at Christmas. I will miss all the times we neighbors have celebrated and mourned the events in our lives together over the years.

My reverie is interrupted by soft fur around my ankles. Stanley, our orange cat, meows. I pick him up and coo, "Be a good boy, Stanley. Take care of your daddy. I love you." Now, Stanley will look after Brady until he comes to England in December, at which time our house sitters will move in.

Brady calls out from the driveway, where he waits with my suit-cases, "Bearess! Let's go."

I hustle out the door and climb into the car. As we drive down Quincy Shore Road, I watch the bay on my right curve and disap-pear as we head onto the Southeast Expressway. I will miss the bay, my walks along the sea wall, and the water's colors, which change depending on the weather and the time of year. What a blessing to live across the street from water. Even in hurricanes, it is beautiful. It will still be here when I return next July, but I have miles to go and unknown experiences waiting for me.

At Boston's Logan International Airport, we settle in for a bit. As we often do when we are in any kind of transition together, Brady and I don't speak for a few minutes; we just sit and hold hands in silence.

Despite people scurrying to and fro, babies fussing and teenagers chattering, we manage to hold this silence between us for a few precious minutes. But flight attendants soon arrive at the gate, and Brady says quietly, "So, Barb, this is it. You're going to England to teach at the Dragon School. I am so thrilled for you! I know this will be a life-changing experience for you, and one I hope you will really embrace with your whole self. Are you ready?"

"I think so! I'm pretty excited but also a little scared. It's been a long process putting this all together, yet I still don't know a lot of what lies ahead. But I guess that's to be expected. When I think about the unknown—"

"Good evening, ladies and gentlemen. Virgin Atlantic is delighted to welcome all passengers on flight VA 1772 nonstop to Gatwick, London. We ask all those who are not on this flight to now leave the boarding area, so we can board everyone in an orderly fashion and depart on time. Thank you," a gate agent announces.

Oh, gosh, it's here—this moment that I've wondered and worried about for the past few weeks as I've packed and unpacked and packed again. How often have I asked myself how I will handle this moment when I have to say goodbye to the man I love, my best friend? Now I don't have time to think about it. That's probably a good thing. I'm not good at goodbyes; I tend to string them out.

Brady takes my hand. "I love you and will miss you and will pray for you. Remember why you are doing this and be strong. I will see you on December nineteenth. And don't forget to call me when you get to Oxford."

"Love you too. Thank you for all your help and for believing in me. I'll miss you very much. Take care of yourself and Stanley. I promise to call when I get to Oxford."

"It's time for me to go," Brady whispers. Not people for public displays of affection, we hug and kiss lightly. We have no more words to say. He waves as he walks out of the boarding area. I watch him go and wave as he disappears into the crowd hurrying here and there. For a nanosecond I want to run to him, to stay here with him, but I know better. That *is not* what I want. What I want with every fiber of my being is to learn how to teach in a whole new way. This is a chance to discover a balance between thinking something should be perfect and knowing when I have done something to the best of my ability.

The flight agent calls out again: "Ladies and gentlemen, we are now boarding rows twenty-nine through thirty-nine. Please have your tickets in hand."

Row twenty-nine? That's me.

Chapter 2
Arduus ad Solem

It's seven o'clock on the morning of September 1, 1998. After a seven-hour flight, my plane lands at Gatwick Airport, twenty miles south of London. Shortly after noon, I arrive at Gloucester Green, the Oxford bus station, and catch a cab. The driver takes me up the Banbury Road into Summertown, and I recognize some of those Cotswold stone houses and gardens from last summer, when I came to Oxford for that poetry class and met Robin Young, head of the Dragon School. I see Gee's, the restaurant where he and I talked about this exchange; a few streets later, my taxi passes Bardwell Road, which leads to the school. I remember walking down this winding, tree-lined street with Robin on that hot July afternoon in 1997, so full of hope and anticipation for this exchange. It seemed so far off in the future, yet here I am, and I already feel a little bit at home.

We pull into Finders Keepers Real Estate's car park. "Here we are, miss," my driver calls out from the front seat of the tiny cab.

I extricate myself from the backseat, grateful that I'm not wearing a short skirt or tight pants, and tell the driver I'll need him to take me to my flat after I pick up the keys.

I open the large glass door and step into a small space with a picture window that floods the office with light and warmth. Three desks sit in the middle of the office; an older man and a young woman work at two of them. A short, plump woman, her hair piled high into a messy bun, tidies magazines and straightens two chairs in the tiny waiting area. As I close the door, she looks up and says, "Hallo! May I be of assistance?"

"Yes, please. I'm here to pick up the keys to the flat I'm letting from you on Hernes Road in Summertown."

She looks pointedly at me and asserts, "We'll need to know your name."

I tell her, and she says, "Let me just have a look at your details." She walks to her desk, sits down, adjusts her hair, and opens a file cabinet.

I try to practice patience as she rifles through papers and takes a phone call. By now, the few minutes I told the cabbie I'd be feel like fifteen. I look outside to see him pacing in the car park.

"Here it is!" she announces and pulls out a rumpled packet of papers. "Now, have a seat and let me go over the lease with you."

I put on my best smile. "Please, may I just sign it and get the keys? My cab is waiting, and I'm really jet lagged. I'll read it and call you if I have any questions."

"I guess that's all right, but you won't be able to ring me—you'll have to come down to the office. There's no phone in the flat."

"No phone in the flat?" I ask, trying not to sound as perturbed as my cabbie outside looks to be.

"Phones are the tenants' responsibility. You can arrange for that by ringing BT [British Telephone]," she quips, and points to a red BT call box across the street.

Too tired to protest, I just want to get to the flat and have a pee. So I take the papers and the keys and try to show appreciation. "Thank you for your help."

Emerging from Finders Keepers, I see my cabbie. He stops pacing, smiles, and opens the door for me. Apologizing for the delay I've caused him, he replies, "No need, ma'am. You look like you've had a long flight and a long day, and all that palaver [British for "BS"] in the letting office didn't help. I'll take you to your flat now."

What a kind man! I sit back, take a deep breath, and exhale my frustrations with the agent.

As we roar up the Banbury Road, my stomach somersaults. *What will my flat look like? Will I like how it's furnished? Who else lives in the building?* Suddenly, we turn onto Hernes Road and I peer more intently out the window. Rounding a bend, we pass a nursing home and several freestanding brick houses. Then a tall brick-and-cinder-block building, set back from the road, with a privet-lined front path, emerges. I see a large sign above the building's steel door with the name WESTGATE engraved in wood above the lintel.

The cabbie parks and comes 'round to open my door, but I'm already on the pavement. He takes my cases out of the cab, refusing to let me carry one. I walk ahead of him to the front door and open it with my key. Flat number 1, my flat, waits at the end of a short, carpeted hallway. I walk along it, past metal mailboxes, to my front door. The cabbie follows with my cases. He seems excited too. "Well, miss, here you are! Your new flat awaits you. Let's make sure the keys work before I drive away."

I hold them—one for the dead bolt and the other for the doorknob—and unlock the door, leaving it ajar. This is a momentous occasion, and I want to enter this place alone. "The keys work fine. You have been very kind. Thank you so much." I pay the fare and give him a generous gratuity.

"Much obliged, ma'am. Thank you!" The driver smiles and tips his cap. I watch him leave the building and turn back to face my flat. *Here goes. Robin picked out this flat for me, so I've no idea what to expect, but I'm going to trust that all will be well.* I take a deep breath and gingerly push open the door into what will be my home for the next eleven months.

My two large suitcases barely fit into the front hallway, which isn't big enough to swing a cat in; it's more like a cubbyhole with some hooks on the wall opposite the door. From the front hall, I am steps away from two bedrooms, which are flooded with bright sunshine. The master bedroom has a large, comfy-looking double bed and two night tables with blue lamps. I turn them on, happy to see I'll have good reading light. Over the bed hangs a large pastel drawing of Canterbury Cathedral, which I remember visiting in 1988. A large picture window framed by blue floral curtains looks out on a small garden. There's also a tall white dresser and wall-to-wall closets in the back of the room. I want to unpack my suitcases right now and settle in, but I should check out the rest of the flat first.

The smaller bedroom has a twin bed with the same blue floral curtains, a tiny closet, a wooden dresser, and a rocking chair that reminds me of my grandmother's rocker in our bedroom back home.

After I put my cases in the spare bedroom, I find the bathroom off another hallway. Amid all the hullabaloo at Finders Keepers, I forgot I needed to pee! I'm halfway to making contact with the seat as I look around for toilet paper. The dispenser is empty. I reach across and open the cabinet under the sink, looking for some, but find none. I pull up my undies, run down the hall, and open a door into a lounge area with a small kitchen, off to the right. I look under the kitchen sink, but no luck. *What is this? They provide cleaning supplies but no toilet paper?* I slam the doors shut and feel a trickle down my thigh. *I can't believe the people at Finders Keepers didn't leave a single roll for me. What am I gonna do?* I waddle back to the bathroom, hoping I don't burst before I reach the pot. Then I think, *My purse!* Holding on more tightly, I hobble to the bedroom and find it. I'm trickling again. I turn the purse upside down and pull out my passport, my wallet, lipstick, and a brown banana I forgot to eat on the plane. Then I find heaven. A wadded-up Kleenex. I lope to the bathroom and take the longest, best-feeling pee ever.

I look for soap to wash my hands. No soap. Nonetheless, I will not be defeated. I rinse my hands, dry them on my skirt, and make a list of groceries I'll need for the next day or two. Then I head back to the Summertown shopping area.

Returning to my flat with groceries, I find a note from Robin Young shoved under the front door of the building, asking me to have dinner with him and his wife tonight. Dinner? Thank goodness for his invitation; I haven't even thought of what I'll do about food!

As I put away the groceries, my jet lag kicks in, and I feel like a wrung-out rag. I straggle into the lounge and plop into one of the blue leather chairs. The day's events race through my mind. *After that marathon trip from Gatwick airport to Oxford, I had to deal with the irritating Finders Keepers agent. Then I got to this flat, which has no phone, no toilet paper, and no soap. I walked down to the Summertown shops and carried back several bags of groceries. Now I have to go back down to town again and call Robin from that stupid call box across from Finders Keepers.*

I pick up the two pillows on the leather chair and fling them, one after the other, with all my might, across the room. They land on the floor under the large picture window. I pick up the pillows and stand to see another small garden right up against the glass. Opening it, I fill my lungs with the freshness of everything around me. Leaning out the window—now I understand why the English don't use screens—I put my nose inside a giant yellow rose and feel my body relax. I step back into the lounge and notice several prints of the English countryside and London Bridge. *This flat isn't so bad; okay, I may not have certain amenities, but I have roses outside my window, and I can buy what I need. I think I'll get some plants and a vase for yellow roses.*

Seeing two people walking down the road with shopping bags reminds me to get back to Summertown to call Robin. Once there, I find the call box.

A familiar voice answers, "The Dragon School, Robin Young speaking."

"Hello, Robin, it's Barbara Kennard. I just found your note."

"Oh! Jolly good! How was your flight over? You must be exhausted from the time change."

"Yes, a bit, but I'm looking forward to seeing you and meeting your wife."

"And how is the flat? Everything in good order? Finders Keepers is an excellent firm."

It won't do to complain about the time I had to wait for the keys, or finding the flat paperless, etc., etc. "It's very comfortable. Thank you so much for locating it. It would have been much more work for me to do that on my own."

"It's a pleasure and the least I could do. I'll let you go; you must have lots to do, and you may want to rest. I'll pick you up at seven o'clock. We'll make it an early evening."

"Thank you. That will be fine. See you then."

I hang up. It's three o'clock now. I can have a shower, take a short nap, unpack a few things, and be ready by seven.

I discover blue bath towels in one of the dresser drawers. After a shower with my new bar of English lavender soap, I pull down the coverlet on the bed in my room to discover it's not made up. Then I realize, *What was I thinking? This isn't a hotel!* I find the sheets in another drawer in the dresser, make the bed, and crawl in. It feels delicious. But after an hour's nap, I wake to an awful realization.

Oh no! I never called Brady. How could I have forgotten to call my husband on the other side of the Atlantic? I need to contact him, but how will I do that? I don't have a phone card or English money to buy one. And I'm still so jet lagged.

Barbara, calm down. Get dressed. Go down to that call box. Call your husband.

I haul one of my suitcases up onto the bed. Looking through the contents for suitable attire to wear to Robin's house for dinner, I see something. *What is this brown and fluffy thing?* I pull on it. Out from under all my clothes and shoes emerges the stuffed bear I gave Brady years ago, with a note attached.

Dear Bearess,

   Since you won't have your real live bear with you, you can have this one to think of me.

   I love you,
   Your Bear

I plop down on the bed and dissolve into tears. *What in God's name made me decide to come all this way by myself? Why did I think I could come over here for four months without Brady? What am I doing here?*

Here without Brady. No phone to call him. Phone. Call. Call box!

I get dressed, grab my purse, and leave the flat. Walking down the Banbury Road, I realize I can use my debit card at the bank's ATM to get some English pounds. I get my money, walk to the call box, and put about five pounds into the coin slot, but then an operator comes on and tells me I can't place a call unless I have an international phone card. I decide to call collect instead. Our phone in Quincy is ringing, when suddenly a car zooms down the Banbury Road and I can't hear a thing. *Oh no—what if Brady picks up the phone while this stupid car is roaring past? I won't be able to hear him answer.*

Suddenly, the noise is gone. I can hear our phone at home ringing again. No answer. More ringing. *Oh no! The answering machine won't take a collect call.* Another ring, and no Brady. *Come on, Brady, pick up! Please, please, answer the phone.*

"Hello?"

"Brady!" I shout into the receiver.

An operator interrupts, "Overseas collect call from Oxford, England. Will you accept?"

"Yes, I will!" Brady says.

"Brady, I'm here! I made it! I'm sorry it took so long to call you. It's been quite a day, but I'm here and I'm okay," I exclaim, jumping up and down inside the call box.

"Hi, Barb! It's so good to hear your voice. How's the flat?"

"Small but cozy." I stoop to pick up coins I've just dropped and almost bump my head on the big metal telephone.

"Good! Listen, I hate to do this, but I was just about to leave for the first faculty meeting of the school year. Can we talk tomorrow or later tonight if you aren't too tired?"

"That's okay. I'm actually going to Robin Young's house for dinner tonight. He's picking me up at seven o'clock. I don't have a phone yet in the flat, but tomorrow I'm going to arrange for one to be installed. I'm using a call box not far from the flat right now."

"I'll be teaching all day tomorrow. Let's see how long it'll take for you to get a phone. Today is Tuesday; if you don't have one by the end of the week, call collect Friday night. That's only three days to wait."

"Okay. I love you and miss you so much. I've had a hard time here today. It's made me wonder what the heck I'm doing here." I glance at a couple walking hand in hand and wipe a few tears from my eyes.

"I miss you too. And remember, you're strong and smart and you *do* know what you're doing there! I've got to go. Love you."

"Love you too. And good luck with the faculty meeting and your classes. Goodbye."

I hang up and step out of the call box. It's almost five o'clock. I have time to walk home, take another shower, and get dressed.

Back at the flat, I quell my hunger with a piece of raisin-and-honey bread I bought at the store in Summertown and some tea—that same tea the Finders Keepers people left me. Guess I know what matters in this country!

Sitting in my lounge with my bear next to me and my tea and bread, I realize Brady is right. I *do* know why I'm here. I'm here because I want something different. I'm here because at this point in my career, I don't believe I can be inspired to do my best teaching in an American school.

My hunger satisfied, my emotions calmer, I wash up my dishes and return to the lounge. Sitting in a big leather chair by the picture window, as my eyes rest on a neighbor's garden across the road, I understand something: I'm also here because *I* need to change. I need to know what I lack to become the teacher God has called me to be, a teacher who can love herself and her students and still challenge them to take intellectual risks, to persevere through difficulties, and to strive for excellence. I want to be more forgiving of myself and others and shed my skin of precision.

Bling, bling, bling, goes my alarm. It's 5:30 a.m. on the morning of September 15, 1998, my first day at the Dragon School. Time to get up. I swing out of bed, but as my feet hit the floor, my legs wobble. Maybe I'm hungry; I'll eat a good breakfast first, then get dressed. In the kitchen, I see the breakfast things I laid out the night before on the dining table in the corner of the lounge: teapot with the tea bag already in it, my teacup, utensils, a place mat, and a napkin. In the kitchen I find the bread on the counter by the toaster, along with the plate for my eggs, bacon, and fruit. I look at the clock on the wall. It's only five forty-five. I make breakfast and eat it as I flip through the lessons I have planned for this first day of classes: some "getting to know you" activities, some reading and writing, some rules of the classroom.

Now it's six thirty. School doesn't start until eight thirty, and it'll take me only about thirty minutes to walk the two miles to campus. *I'll take a shower. . . . Wait, I showered last night.* I decide to do my breakfast dishes, rather than put them in the dishwasher for later, and fill the sink with dish soap and warm water. As I finish the dishes, I smell something and look around to see the piece of toast I forgot to eat smoking in the toaster. Yikes! I grab a dish towel, snatch the bread, unplug the toaster from the wall, and toss the crispy black mess into the trash. *Phew! That was close!*

Next, I head to the guest bedroom, where I laid out my school clothes last night, but first I brush my teeth, wash my face, and do my makeup. My heart races as I finish up my ablutions. I take some deep breaths and get dressed. My legs shake. Maybe I should sit down for a minute. All dressed and ready to go, I look at my watch. *Damn, it's only seven thirty. If I leave for school now, I'll get there at eight. I'll take out the trash and clean the flat a bit.*

I arrive at school at 8:10 and walk through the school's rickety wooden gate to find a crowd of children running, shouting, and playing marbles in the schoolyard. It's an oddly shaped area enclosed on one side by a cinder-block library and some two-story classrooms with large picture windows. On the opposite side of the schoolyard sit more classrooms, the school auditorium, a modern structure made of metal, and a "games box" with sports equipment spilling over its rim. Alone at the back end of the schoolyard, a sleek iron bell rises from the asphalt pavement. This is definitely different from Fessenden—no flower beds or stately redbrick buildings—but the kids seem lively and happy, and, given some of the school buildings I've taught in, I know not to judge one based on what first meets the eye.

Out of all this quagmire, one tousled-haired student wearing the Dragon uniform of navy-blue shorts and a yellow shirt pops up and calls out, "Hallo, Ma Kennard! You must be the American teacher come to take Mr. Cameron's place. What are you going to teach us?"

This boy's forthrightness dashes my stereotypes of the English. Indeed, the rest of the school community exhibits similar warmth and friendliness. Teachers and staff ask how I'm coping: "Are you getting along all right so far from home?" "Do you need anything for your classroom?" Neither the children nor the adults at Dragon embody the "reserve" or the "wait until you're spoken to" clichés I've formally associated with English people.

A young Dragon rings the school bell at 8:25 a.m. Time for morning assembly. All of us—students, teachers, administrators, and staff—run, walk, or meander into Lyman's Hall. One of the administrators welcomes everyone back and reads a few announcements from the stage. The school chaplain tells a poignant story relating to the school motto, *Arduus ad Solem* ("Striving Towards the Sun"), and seven hundred people sing the school song, "Jerusalem."

The headmaster introduces me: "Ma Kennard has exchanged jobs with Mr. Cameron, who has gone to Boston to teach her classes at the

Fessenden School. She will be teaching English and Drama. Please help her find her way around the school and make her feel welcome. Upper 2B, process with Ma Kennard to first-period class."

In a matter of seconds, twenty-five thirteen-year-old boys and girls lope out of the auditorium, grab their rucksacks (backpacks), and clamber around me.

The lobby is packed with kids and teachers all trying to make their way to their respective classrooms. Teachers shout, "Get to class!" My stomach churns. Twenty-five kids? Thirteen-year-olds? In all my years of teaching, I've never had twenty-five students in a class, let alone taught thirteen-year-olds.

I pull out my "I'm in charge" teacher voice and declare, "Good morning, Upper 2B. We will be in classroom C in the 'tin can.'" They run, and I walk as fast as I can, across the cement playground to the aluminum building where my class will reside for the year while new classroom space is constructed.

Before I can get there, the door to my room bangs shut. Louis opens it with a charming smile and apologizes, "Sorry, Ma." Then he scolds the others: "Hey, you lot left Ma Kennard outside. That wasn't nice!"

"Sorry, Ma!" all twenty-five of them chorus. Then they begin to romp about the room. A few climb on the desks. This class has real zeal, but I'm not sure if it's because of the *Alice in Wonderland* posters I've placed on the wall, or if they're testing the new teacher, and an American one at that. Then I wonder something a little scarier: Is this how all Dragon students act? I guess I'll just have to find out!

Our dingy yellow classroom needs more light than one fluorescent bulb can offer. I ask Harry, a tall boy who seems at odds about whether to join his mates on top of the desks, to open the dark blue curtains.

"Yes, Ma," he states, and strides across the room in two steps. The rest of the class stops their noise at his obedience.

"Thank you, Harry. Now, if the rest of you will sit down, we'll get started with class." I say, walking over to an old metal teacher's desk positioned in front of twenty-five metal student desks.

A raft of hands wave at me, accompanied by a chorus of enthusiastic shouting: "Ma Kennard, what's your school like in the States? What's New York City like? What music do you listen to?"

"I know you have lots of questions. Please sit down and raise your hands, and I will call on you one at a time," I say.

They quiet down a bit but are still somewhat rambunctious, fighting, talking, and giggling in the back rows.

I wait.

They settle.

I spend part of every class of my first day at the Dragon answering questions about who I am, where I live, and what I like to do.

As Robin and I discussed last summer, I teach ninety-five kids from "across the school" every day. My youngest class, Lower 2A, a lively bunch of nine-year-olds, ranks second in ability from the top of their age group. Next, Middle 3B, an easygoing group of ten-year-olds, are in fourth out of seventh place in their age group. My eleven-year-olds, Upper 5, a wise collection of scholars, are at the top of their age group. My oldest class, Upper 2B, the raucous but endearing assortment of thirteen-year-olds with whom I start my day, also stand in fourth out of seven places in their age group.

Despite their general rowdiness, my students endear themselves to me with their enthusiasm and curiosity about America and me. But we will need to build a partnership, so I ask each class what rules we will live by. They all seem to understand some of the same values. I compile each class's list and a few of my own.

Theirs:

Raise hands.

Be nice to each other.

Respect the teacher.

Mine:

Come to class prepared.

Respect different opinions.

Participate.

Thus, we begin our "honeymoon period."

It doesn't seem to matter if it's in Boston, Massachusetts, or Oxford, England—students want to reveal their best selves in the early weeks of the school year. But, as with most honeymoons, this initial felicity doesn't last.

Mine ends when I walk into my classroom one blustery day in late September to find Upper 2B clowning around like characters from the '60s English film *To Sir, with Love.* I shut the door, and my dragons land in their assigned seats lickety-split, then fall silent. They start on the assignment I wrote on the board for them the day before. They're too quickly engrossed in their writing; something's afoot.

I put my books on my desk, take off my hat and coat, and hang them on the hook next to the whiteboard behind my desk. Turning back to my desk chair, I see what isn't right.

"Oh, look what we have here!"

My students continue to stare at the essays they're supposed to be writing, but a few snickers rise from the back row.

I hold up a yardstick with a large brown plastic turd dangling off the end of it.

Plop goes the pile in the trash can. "Carry on writing your essays. I'll collect them at the end of class," I say, as I sit in my turd-free chair.

Taking out my lesson book, I pretend to write out plans for next week and try to imagine what to say to these kids. My students at Fessenden wouldn't *dare* such a rude gesture.

The silence in my classroom draws me out of myself. I look up to see the entire class at work on their essays. Their contrition is palpable. Something tells me not to respond to this prank right now. The students are focused on their work, and that should be the priority.

At bun break, I talk to my mentor, Jenny Simmons, who is about my age and has been at the Dragon for six years. She teaches science to Upper 2B across the hall from me. After I explain the turd scenario, Jenny offers some insight: "Such a joke is not uncommon at Dragon, especially with new teachers, but I shouldn't get your knickers in a twist over it. This form is a challenge for me too, but I find it works best if I don't make too much out of some of their sillier antics, so I can make a bigger deal of the things that matter, like when they don't do their science prep."

Jenny's response relieves me. I also notice her use of "shouldn't," instead of "wouldn't"—an example of a difference between English and American English, the former more direct but said with a hint of humor.

The next day, Upper 2B comes to class without their usual noise and chaos. Instead, they slink into their seats and avoid looking at me. I've made them wait long enough for my response to their turd, so I say, "Upper 2B, you probably know that I was pretty surprised yesterday at your prank. I have to say that I found it upsetting, as a guest at your school, to be treated in such a manner."

Silence. The kids look at each other. A few fumble with their rucksacks.

Slowly, I walk around to the front of my desk and sit on it. The kids look at me with apprehension. I wouldn't call it fear, but they're certainly on tenterhooks about what I might do next. Actually, by now the whole episode seems kind of funny to me. Instead of quelling my anger, I have to suppress a smile. *Keep a stiff upper lip, Barbara.*

Sitting on the desk, ankles crossed and hands resting in my lap, I say, in a voice a little louder than a whisper, "Students like to test their teacher. I did that when I was a kid, though I don't think I put a plastic turd on a teacher's chair. I guess I should be grateful that it wasn't real!"

The whole room erupts into howls, and even I join in. Then little Daisy, with her blond braids, who looks like she's five, instead of thirteen, coos, "Ma Kennard, we'd never do *that*! We just wanted to see what you'd do."

"Okay. Well, I hope that impulse is out of your system. Let's get to work on some grammar. Take out your practice booklets and work on diagramming these sentences." I jump off my desk and pull up an antique map of Britain to reveal ten sentences. Twenty-five metal desktops creak open, and they rustle about for pens and their little orange grammar books. Then a sudden quiet prevails as my dragons get to work. They don't engage in the usual silliness they bring into class each day, and they may sense that I'll have one more word. Although they don't apologize, their remorse is evident.

As the class period ends, I walk to the door. They collect their rucksacks like little soldiers. Gathering around me, these thirteen-year-olds look touchingly like little boys and girls. "Upper 2B, I can see that you feel bad about what you did, but I have forgiven you. Don't let it bother you anymore; let us put this behind us and move forward," I say as I open the door.

My dragons fly out the door, shouting, "Thanks, Ma. You're a brilliant [cool] teacher!"

During bun break a few days later, teachers chat in the common room over coffee and cheese buns while the kids have their recess. I glance out the window at children running helter-skelter all over the schoolyard, rolling around on the asphalt, and roughhousing with each other. Others play hopscotch and jacks on one side of the yard. At Fessenden, there'd be three or four teachers standing around while the boys played football or soccer. I ask Jenny, "Are the kids okay without a teacher watching them at recess?"

Jenny replies with a smile, "Oh, yes, no need to worry. They play rough, but no one ever gets really hurt. They know they're responsible for each other and that we teachers are having our bun break as well. By the way, how are things going since that incident in your room?"

I pour more coffee into each of our mugs and tell her, "Oh, fine. I had a good heart-to-heart talk with them the other day. Things are lighter now."

Jenny swirls sugar into her coffee and looks at me with a bit of a smirk, as if to ask, *That's all you have to say about this incident?*

I take her point. "You know, despite their naughtiness, I think Upper 2B meant their prank as a harmless bit of fun. Based on their demeanor after my comments about it, I don't think they'll do something like that again."

My mentor laughs and almost chokes on her biscuit. "I should hope not!" She points to some chairs that two other colleagues have vacated. We sit, and Jenny continues, "You handled the situation brilliantly. If you were upset, for which I wouldn't blame you, you certainly kept it close to your chest, so as not to give the children the impression they had come out on top."

The first of three bells signals the end of bun break. Four or five teachers put down their coffee, stuff the remains of biscuits into their mouths, and head to their next class. Jenny and I do not teach next period. This is our weekly mentor meeting time, so I continue, "I've been observing how you handle the kids' behavior here. There seems to be a more forgiving tone toward pranks like the one pulled on me. Dragon accepts that children will engage in such antics by virtue of the very fact that they're children. At Fessenden, we'd have a more formal response; a meeting would be held with the children's parents, the principal, and the teacher, and the children would be admonished and given chores as restitution."

"We don't have time for that, but I'm sure there are other differences between Dragon and Fessenden," Jenny says, as two dining staff come in and begin to clean up the common room. Jenny puts her coffee mug on the nearby cart and stands up. "I admire how you take all this in your stride, Barbara."

"Thank you, Jenny." She motions to the coat rack, and we suit up for the walk back to our classrooms. As we leave Gunga Din, I offer, "The turd incident has helped me recognize some of my strengths and weaknesses that I might not have discovered had I not come to the Dragon. That's why I'm here."

"And we are glad you are!" Then she asks graciously, "Since this is our usual meeting time, do you have other things on your mind?"

"No, I don't think so. You've been very encouraging. You're very generous with your time."

"It's a pleasure, Barbara!" she says with genuine delight. "I'll leave you to it, then, and finish some marking I should have done last night."

"Right!" I wave at Jenny as she crosses the schoolyard to her classroom. Thinking about our conversation about the kids' prank, I practically skip to the curriculum library to check out materials for my M3B class. It's so good to have Jenny as a mentor; she helps me see the humor in situations I might otherwise take too seriously. And that inspires me to hold back from carrying on about what I'm learning about myself here. That isn't the English way. And it would never do to tell Upper 2B how humiliated I felt about their behavior. If the Dragon doesn't worry about such shenanigans, maybe I don't need to either. Not only here, but back at Fessenden too.

By mid-October, Upper 2B and I are enjoying a strong rapport. We read some Kafka short stories and parts of *Frankenstein*. Knowing my students' penchant for "larking about," I suggest we dramatize some scenes from *The Tempest*. Upper 2B's restraint with the shipwreck scene surprises me; there's a good chance they could lose control when the ship is tossed about and the passengers freak out, but the kids choreograph a messy and scary scene with plenty of noise and confusion that is surprisingly safe. After their efforts, I compliment them: "Upper 2B, your scene was brilliant but not over the top. I felt like I was on a sinking ship! Well done!"

Of course, being Upper 2B, they also want to do the drunk-en-butler scene in Act 3, when Trinculo and Stephano stumble into Caliban. This scene is one of the play's great comic moments: The two men attempt to get Caliban drunk so the three of them can remove Prospero from power and take control of the island themselves. I wonder how they'll manage this one, but the students perform this classic funny episode by focusing on Shakespeare's verse, rather than by acting like stereotypical drunks. I suppose this is due to their being English—meter is in their blood. Some of the girls also create a kind of mythical, slow-motion interpretation of the wedding masque, singing their lines and dancing about the room.

Watching this wonder unfold in my classroom, I understand

something for the first time: Reading Shakespeare's beautiful poetry excites students. They don't require information about themes, characters, and conflicts. These students are encouraged to work diligently at something without necessarily having all the information that's available to them.

I realize from this experience that I often have given students too much material to digest, information that they are not developmentally or intellectually ready for but that makes me, the administration, and some of my students and their parents happy that the children look smart, even if they don't understand what they're doing. But the Dragon respects students' various developmental stages and doesn't expect them to do more than what makes sense for their age and ability. Equally important for the students' enjoyment, playing with Shakespeare or any other literature doesn't turn into polished performances for parents or any audience; it's simply an opportunity for the students to have some fun with schoolwork that engages and excites them.

Chapter 3
Glimpsing God

As I adjust to teaching at the Dragon, I also begin to make myself at home in Oxford, the city of "dreaming spires," so named for the magnificent towers that rise out of the daily morning mist and fog. On Saturdays after morning classes, I often walk to the Covered Market, a continuous fixture of the city since 1774. Vendors arrive each Saturday morning to sell a range of international foods, household goods, unique clothing, organically grown produce, luscious ice cream, and bakery items. Everything for sale has been handmade or grown by people from the Oxfordshire countryside. The place is loud, smelly, and crowded. Sometimes I run into Dragon students and their families. and I delight in hearing them call out, "Hallo, Ma Kennard!" I respond with a smile and maybe a greeting, but half Saturdays are precious time off; no one wants to stop and chat.

At the market, I usually treat myself to lunch at one of the many unique places to eat. Today, I try the Greek Taverna for some moussaka. After lunch I stroll around, getting lost in the aisles. I buy some organic leeks, an organic chicken, which is plucked and feathered right in front of me, and a pair of hand-knitted gloves. After pistachio ice cream at Danny's Creamery and more wandering about, I catch the number 7 bus back to my flat in Summertown.

On any given Saturday in Boston, Brady and I would scamper

around, cleaning the house, doing laundry and food shopping, and would be exhausted by evening. But even though I teach on Saturday mornings here, I actually feel as if I have more time after classes are over because the pace of life is slower here.

One particular Saturday in late October, I arrive home from marketing to meet my upstairs neighbor, Jacqui Gill. Tall and slim, with piercing blue eyes, she glares at me in the front hallway of our building. She also speaks first: "Are you the new tenant in flat one?"

I put my groceries on a bench under the mailboxes. "Yes, I just moved in. My name's Barbara Kennard." I extend my hand.

Jacqui shakes my hand and exclaims, "Oh, you're an American!"

I take a step back at her greeting. I'm not sure why she speaks loudly; does Jacqui dislike Americans, or is she enthusiastic about having one as a neighbor? And yet she did initiate our conversation and shake my hand. I step closer to her and say, "Yes, I'm from Boston, and I'm here on a teaching exchange at the Dragon School."

"I love America! I lived there in the eighties and still go back. In fact, I've just returned from a visit to see friends in Alexandria, Virginia."

"Were you there for work?" I ask.

"I was secretary to the Dean of the Episcopal Cathedral in Washington, DC, for five years. Why don't you come for tea at half three? I'm in flat four, just above you," she offers.

I pick up my groceries and thank Jacqui. "I'd love to! See you then."

As I walk to my flat at the end of the hallway, I watch Jacqui climb the concrete stairs to the second floor and unlock her front door. In my kitchen, I muse over her ways as I unpack my groceries. I think about her forthrightness and remember, as I did when I first saw the Dragon School buildings, not to pass judgment on the way things are here. Maybe Jacqui had this experience while she was in the States and brought some Americanisms back with her. Perhaps I'll do the same when I return home.

After spending time marking student papers, I notice the time. Yikes! It's 3:35! I put my papers in order and bolt upstairs to Jacqui's flat. She opens the door immediately and stands in the middle of her entry with one hand on her hip. Funny how the English can be so obsessed with punctuality, yet they tolerate the long queues and wait times for just about everything and anything as a fact of life.

"Do come in, Barbara, and take a seat." Jacqui ushers me to a faded but cozy Queen Anne chair, next to which rests a small side table set with a blue-and-white tea mug, a small matching plate, and a petite napkin. I have only a minute to survey her lounge but notice posters of New York and Chicago and some English countryside prints on her walls. Jacqui comes in from her kitchen and places a wooden tray with a small silver teapot and matching cream-and-sugar containers on the table between us. The room is warm, sunlit. Though sparsely furnished with only two other chairs and a large oak table, her lounge feels comfortable and homey.

"Milk? Sugar?" Jacqui queries.

"Yes, please—a little of both."

I watch her pour a bit of milk into my cup. She then adds tea and hands me the sugar bowl. I help myself to a small cube with the tiny tongs from the tray. "This tea is lovely, Jacqui. Such a nice thing to have on this cold October day."

Jacqui notices how I sip the steaming aromatic brew. "Is your tea too hot? I can add some cold water or milk."

"It's just right, thank you." Then I venture another question: "Does pouring the milk in first make it taste better? When my husband and I have tea at home in Boston, we put the milk in after we pour the tea, but I like your way better."

Jacqui purses her lips and arches one eyebrow, an indication that I've said something offensive or amusing; trouble is, I don't know which it is unless the person explains, which the English don't always do. Fortunately, in this case, my words aren't egregious to her.

"Oh, you are funny and so American!"

"I guess being funny and American are good things?" I ask, settling into my chair.

"Quite! I do love Americans. But sometimes the way you all think is rather comical. I guess it's obvious to us why we pour the milk with tea as we do. It's all about class. The rich pour after because they use bone china, and the lower class pours before so as to not break their ceramic cups."

"Oh, I see."

"Biscuit?" Jacqui holds out a plate of four chocolate-covered biscuits.

"These look delicious," I remark, but hold back from taking more than one. I know that even if there are two for each of us, as a guest, I should wait for my English hostess to offer the next one.

Jacqui notices me looking at her small wooden cross that hangs over her front window and says, "May I ask, are you a Christian?"

Her question feels forward coming from someone I've just met. I cast my eyes downward for a second. "Yes, I guess you could say that I am, though I haven't been to church in several years," I admit, and look at a floral print on the far wall.

Jacqui picks up her teapot. "More tea?" I turn to her and nod. Quietly she says, "You must have had good reason for staying away from church."

I look down at the blue-and-red herringbone rug beneath my feet before I say, "Well, yes, we did—that is, my husband, Brady, and I did. We left our Episcopal church in Boston in 1996 because it modernized the service to appeal to those who were unfamiliar with its liturgy and music. The addition of guitar music and the removal of some of the traditional language from the prayers didn't appeal to us. We just didn't feel at home after those changes were made," I say, and sip more tea.

"Oh, I do understand! I loved the cathedral in Washington for its classical worship and music." Jacqui offers the plate of biscuits to me again.

I take one more and say, "We looked around for another church, but by the time I had to leave for my exchange here, we hadn't found one we felt called to."

For a moment we both bask in the late-afternoon light flooding Jacqui's lounge. Then she offers, "This light reminds me of some of the prayers we pray at Evensong. I'm going to that service at Christ Church Cathedral tomorrow afternoon at five o'clock. Why not come with me?"

"What's an Evensong?"

Jacqui leans toward me and says, "It's an ancient Anglican worship service held at the end of the day. I think you'll enjoy it because much of the service includes traditional Anglican music sung by the choir and the clergy. I'm sure you'll recognize some of the hymns, since you've attended an Episcopal church in the States. Anglican and Episcopal worship are in many ways one and the same."

Jacqui's description of Evensong takes me back to Trinity Church in Boston. I can see parishioners in the pews, and some of our friends seated near us. Communion is over, and the congregation stands for the final prayer of Thanksgiving. The celebrant gives a blessing, and the organist plays the recessional hymn, "Repton." The crucifer and acolytes lead the choir down the center aisle as three hundred people sing, "Breathe through the heats of our desire thy coolness and thy balm; let sense be dumb, let flesh retire, speak through the earth-quake, wind, and fire, o still small voice of calm. . . ." This hymn, even here in Jacqui's lounge, reveals a God who doesn't have to get our attention with force. Indeed, God also comes to us in song, like a bird in flight back to Earth.

But I shouldn't share this revelation to my new friend, at least not so early in our acquaintance. English people don't do that. While I know my English friends and colleagues don't expect me to be just like them, they expect me to be almost like them. Even so, Jacqui seems to understand how much traditional liturgy means to me, and her invitation is freely offered. I don't feel pressured, as I have in the past when friends in Boston kept asking me to go to church with them week after week. Jacqui smiles as she cocks her head to one side. I tell her, "Evensong sounds lovely. What time should I be ready tomorrow?"

"Brilliant! It will take at least thirty minutes to walk to the cathedral, and the pews fill up quickly. We should leave here at four o'clock sharp," she says with a grin, and stands up.

I take this as my cue to leave, which I need to do anyway. "Right! I'll be ready. It was kind of you to have me for tea, but I should get back to my flat. I have a lot of student papers to mark before Monday."

Jacqui gives me a wide smile, and her eyes sparkle. She walks me to her door and extends her hand. "A pleasure to have you. See you tomorrow."

Back in my flat, I think about Jacquie's invitation and recall her suggestion that I'll recognize some of the hymns. My thoughts turn back to our church in Boston, where I can hear the thoughtful and unpreachy words of bible study; indeed, Brady and I met in one of those classes and were married in that church.

I swallow hard and remind myself that I have work to do, but after

I've marked a few papers, something wells up from deep in my stomach. I run to the loo, but nothing comes up or out.

Did I eat something bad at Jacqui's? Is this homesickness?

No, it's neither of these things.

I know what it is.

The words that have been waiting to speak for a long time flow from the pit of my gut, past my heart, into my throat, and out of my mouth. "Oh, God, I am so sorry that I left the church, that I stopped reading the Bible and singing hymns to myself. I want to ask for your forgiveness."

Tears come hard and fast. I stumble to the bedroom. The big, soft teddy bear Brady gave me sits on my pillow, gazing at me. I climb up on my bed, take hold of my bear, and begin to sing part of a favorite hymn: "Be thou my vision, O Lord of my heart . . . Waking or sleeping, Thy presence, my light." I can't remember all the words, but it soothes me to sing what I know over and over.

I'm suddenly hungry. Eating supper of soup and salad, I have a revelation: *Maybe God noticed me staring at Jacqui's cross. Maybe her suggestion to go to Evensong wasn't a coincidence. I used to think coincidences were things that just happen on their own, but I don't think that's true. Coincidences are important. If we pay careful attention to them, we might notice something other than the coincidence itself; maybe there's more going on than what meets the eye. Like a presence of some kind. We should take time to see what might be waiting in the wings of a coincidence.*

After supper, I return to my schoolwork but again am distracted. I'm worried I might cry at the service tomorrow. How will I contain myself if I'm moved to tears? I can't let this happen. It's not like we'll be in my former church in Boston with people I know and where I sometimes cried over a hymn I love; we'll be in Christ Church

Cathedral with tons of English people who have a good grip on their emotions. I hardly know Jacqui; if I cry during Evensong, it could make her uncomfortable, and I'd feel awkward because a particular hymn caused something powerful to well up inside me. Maybe I shouldn't go. Maybe it would be better to take my usual Sunday walk in Port Meadow. I often walk there for hours on Sunday, my one free day away from school. That settles it: I'll tell Jacqui in the morning that I can't go to Evensong because I have too much schoolwork to do.

On Sunday I enjoy the deliciousness of sleeping until 9:00 a.m. Oxford sits in a valley, and when it's foggy, which is much of the time, Oxfordians describe it as a damp, dark, and dismal place. But when I spread open my bedroom window curtains this morning, I see the sun! After a breakfast of poached eggs, bacon, toast, and tea, I dress in cotton pants, my walking boots, and several layers of cotton tops for my jaunt in Port Meadow. And I grab my brolly (umbrella). We all bring brollies when walking around Oxford, "for the rain it raineth [almost] every day."

I walk down my street and turn onto the Banbury Road. Just before reaching the city center, I turn left into the University Parks and Gardens and amble among students sprinkled everywhere, dressed in shorts and T-shirts, reading and talking with each other. At the other end of the parks and gardens, I come to the little village of Jericho, a neighborhood of Oxford. From here I wander along the River Isis, passing a community of colorful houseboats, to an old steel bridge that rises high over the water. Climbing the bridge one step at a time, I pause at its summit to take in the wide-open meadow and a 365-degree view of Oxford. Sweaty and warm from the sun, I strip off my top layer of clothing. Next, I take the muddy path across the meadow to the ruins of a twelfth-century stone church. Past the remains of the West Window, the path divides. The left leads to the Trout Inn, a seventeenth-century pub. The right takes me into the center of the meadow, where it is all mine, save a myriad of birds flitting about and the occasional beaver making its dam. This place is church to me. God forgive me for leaving the church, but sites like this are mysterious and holy in their own way, with all this wildness and silence.

After meandering for several hours, I stop at one of the sandwich shops back in Jericho for something to eat. In the café, the wall clock chimes two. Oh my gosh! I forgot to tell Jacqui I won't be going to Evensong with her this afternoon. I can't just not show up. I have to tell her I have too much schoolwork to do. I run-walk as fast as I can back to my building, barely making it up the stairs to Jacqui's flat. I stand before her door. I hear her walking toward it. I raise my hand. But before I can knock, Jacqui opens it.

"Oh, hallo, Barbara. I was just down to your flat to see if you'd like to come for tea before we go to Evensong. I always get a bit peckish during the service unless I have tea before I go. You've been out walking, from the looks of you! It's already a quarter to three; why not get dressed for Evensong and come back up for some tea at half three?"

Without skipping a beat, I reply, "That would be lovely, Jacqui. Thank you." I bolt down the stairs into my flat, tear off my sweaty clothes, and hop into a hot shower, where I converse with my conscience:

Why did I so quickly say yes to Jacqui when I intended to tell her I couldn't go to Evensong?

Because maybe you really do want to go back to church.

But I really should stay home and finish my schoolwork.

You took a walk in Port Meadow instead of marking student papers. If you'd done your work, you'd be able to go to Evensong.

To tell the truth, I don't want to go because I'm afraid the hymns and prayers will make me feel bad that I left the church.

But your excuse to Jacqui was about doing your schoolwork.

I couldn't tell her how I feel about leaving the church.

You just asked God to forgive you for leaving the church.

That's true, but I'm more comfortable in a place like Port Meadow when it comes to worshipping God.

But you admit you also love the hymns and prayers of the church.

That's also true.

You could do both.

Okay, I'll go to Evensong and try to keep it together.

Staring at the few "dress" clothes I brought with me from Boston, I wonder if there's a certain type of outfit one wears for Evensong. A gray-and-navy plaid skirt with a navy sweater seems appropriate, along with a pair of silver earrings and my grandmother's crystal necklace.

After tea, Jacqui and I walk to Christ Church. We arrive in time to hear the bells of Tom Tower ringing for the service to begin and make our way through the spacious quad to the entrance of the church. This Norman cathedral, begun in the thirteenth century and finished by Cardinal Wolsey in the sixteenth, is the cathedral for the city of Oxford and the chapel of Christ Church College. Jacqui escorts me through the ancient stone door into the spacious nave, with its vaulted ceiling and collection of cushion-lined chairs. Looking up and all around me, I'm rooted in place as I gaze at the panorama of Wolsey's masterpiece. Intricately carved figures of saints, prophets, and gargoyles balance at the end of stone ribs that jut out from the sides of the cathedral ceiling. They stare down at me from on high. Below this magnificent canopy hundreds of stained-glass windows tell stories of the Bible, of English history, and of the divine right of kings. Taking it all in, I think, *I have never felt so small, and yet how else can one feel when enveloped by such glory?*

Evensong begins with the processional hymn, one I don't know, but I stand with the rest of the congregation and try to sing along. The boy choir processes up the center aisle behind the tall gold crucifix, followed by two priests. The first wears a luxurious green-and-gold-trimmed robe, and the second one, a simple white robe with a green stole. The service begins with the call to worship. Then we sit and listen to the choir sing their first anthem. After that, someone from the congregation climbs into the baroque-style carved lectern and reads an Old Testament lesson. The choir sings another anthem, and another member of the congregation reads the New Testament lesson. Both readings are from the King James Bible.

So far, most of the music is unfamiliar to me, so I haven't worried about getting too emotional over it, but now I may be in trouble because I know this next piece well; Brady and I used to hear it at Trinity. Sung a cappella in a four-part canon, Richard Farrant's anthem, "Lord, for Thy Tender Mercy's Sake," is characteristic of the beautiful lyricism and poetry of English Renaissance choral music. I am never sure if it's the music, the words of this hymn, or both that touch me so deeply every time I hear it.

> *Lord, for thy tender mercy's sake,*
> *lay not our sins to our charge,*
> *but forgive what is past,*
> *and give us grace to amend our sinful lives:*
> *to decline from sin and incline to virtue,*
> *that we may walk in a perfect heart*
> *before thee, now and evermore.*
> *Amen.*

Listening to this anthem, I swallow hard and sniffle a bit. Without saying a word, Jacqui passes me a tissue. I take it, gently pat her hand, and collect myself by looking at the stained-glass windows, still so colorful four centuries later. I also see that people from different parts of the world are here. A woman in a sari gazes up at the vaulted ceiling. Two young Africans behind me whisper in a Nigerian accent about the ornate altar. Along the side aisle, two older women wearing bright Spanish-style dresses walk toward a reliquary.

The choir finishes the Farrant. We kneel along with the priests and choir to chant the Lord's Prayer. The officiant sings the absolution and remission of sins, and we stand to chant the General Thanksgiving, that magnificent poem of gratitude for "our creation, preservation, and all the blessings of this life." After that, the deacon speaks the dismissal, "Let us bless the Lord," and the congregation responds with "Thanks be to God." Finally, the organist begins a favorite recessional hymn, "Praise My Soul, the King of Glory." With joy and confidence, I lift my voice and sing.

Jacqui and I leave the cathedral and take the bus home. Inside the foyer of our building, we say good night.

"Barbara, I'm so glad you could come to Evensong with me."

"I'm glad I went too. It was a beautiful service."

"Perhaps you'd like to go again?"

"I think so."

"Good night, Barbara. Have a good sleep."

"You too, Jacqui, and thank you for taking me."

It's almost 7:00 p.m. I heat up some leftovers, set the table, and pour myself a glass of wine. Then I do something I haven't done in a while: Instead of asking for help, I thank God out loud. "Thank you, God, for Jacqui and for Evensong. I'm so grateful I could enjoy the service without losing myself in tears. Being there made me realize how much I miss the prayers and music I've loved since I was a child. I want to go back to church to have more experiences of your mysterious presence and power."

Cleaning up my dinner dishes, I realize how much I want to share my Evensong experience with Brady when we next talk, especially the music and how deeply satisfying it felt to sing some hymns we both know and love. And he'll like knowing about the cathedral's architecture and the stained-glass windows.

The beginning of October passes quickly as the days grow shorter. Now I walk the two miles to school in early dawn and back to my flat at sunset. My afternoon walk reminds me of the many times Brady and I strolled around our neighborhood in Quincy in that same twilight. We loved watching the lights come on in people's houses as the afternoon darkened, and we joked about our innocent voyeurism. "I like seeing people when they can't see me!" he would say, and I'd respond, "It's fun to imagine what they're saying to each other or what they're eating for dinner." I miss Brady, but I've been here now for two months and I'm coping without him pretty well. I'm making friends and feeling better acquainted with Oxford. I do miss roaming around Boston with my American friends, but we write each other from time to time. Moreover, it won't help me to maintain my equilibrium if I call Brady every time I miss him. Besides, he's adjusting nicely in my absence, through his latest project—to learn more of his beloved Beethoven piano sonatas—and by socializing with friends. It feels good to be able to carry on without him. We send emails, but sometimes they get lost in cyberspace, so we wait for our Saturday-afternoon phone dates, when hearing each other's voice makes us feel closer. Today, it's my turn to call him.

"Brady! It's so good to hear your voice."

"Same here. How are things going?"

"Really well. School feels pretty routine now; it doesn't feel like it's all new to me anymore. But I've had a couple of new things happen outside of school that I'm excited to share with you. I'm getting to know one of my neighbors. Her name is Jacqui. She's had me for tea, and last Sunday she took me to an Evensong service at Christ Church Cathedral."

"How nice; I'm glad you're connecting with new people. When I was a student at the Royal College of Music in London, some of my housemates attended Evensong services, but I never went to one. Did you like it?"

I sip some tea and say, "I did. First of all, the cathedral is an amazing place. It's huge, much bigger than any church we've been to in Boston, including Trinity. It's so old, you can sense the centuries of worship that have happened there. And the music is just gorgeous. I loved the whole service."

"What did they do in the service? Was it like the ones we enjoyed at Trinity before it went modern?"

"Well, for one thing, the entire service, except for the reading of the lessons, is sung by the boys' choir, accompanied by a few adult men. Their singing made me feel like I was in the presence of something holy."

"No doubt you were."

I hear our cat purring; he must be on Brady's lap, "I felt that especially when the choir was singing that anthem we love and that we used to hear the Trinity choir sing, the one by Richard Farrant—"

"You mean, 'Lord, for Thy Tender Mercy's Sake'?"

"Yes, that's the one. Anyway, I kind of lost it when they sang it. It was so beautiful, and it took me back to our days at Trinity. It makes me want to return to church and to being part of a faith community."

"What do you mean when you say you 'kind of lost it'?"

"I cried. Well, I didn't really cry; it was more like a bit of weeping. I can't explain it very well."

"What words made you teary?"

"Probably the idea of declining from sin and walking with a perfect heart. I ask God to forgive my sins, but I don't walk with a perfect heart."

"Don't be too hard on yourself, Barb. None of us can walk with a perfect heart in this life. The point is not to be perfect but to be faithful. All God asks of us is to keep trying to be our best selves, little by little. You might be applying your perfectionism here a bit. Only God is perfect—we are not!"

"I guess you're right. But I think it will help to be part of a faith community again. I want to find a church we like in Boston when we return next year."

"I'd like that too. Being here in Boston makes me realize what I'm missing, besides being with you. I miss the interaction with people of faith that we had at Trinity, and I think we lose something when we aren't part of church life." I hear Brady's leather recliner crunch as he continues, "I remember all those covenant groups and Bible studies with folks from Trinity and how we were there for each other in difficult and good times, like when some of our friends got married or when Helen was diagnosed with cancer. Everyone in our covenant group prayed and cooked and rejoiced together."

"I remember those times too. I've got my *Book of Common Prayer* here. Let's end our call with one of my favorite prayers." I open my book and read that wonderful blessing from Isaiah, "O God, you will keep in perfect peace those whose minds are fixed on you; for in returning and rest we shall be saved; in quietness and trust shall be our strength."

We say "Amen" together.

Before we hang up, we discuss my upcoming holiday from school. I have a delicious ten days to do whatever I want. Besides hanging out in Oxford, Brady encourages me to explore England a bit. Over the course of my day, I consider my options, and I find myself craving a landscape that is completely different from the flat and fog of Oxford—something hilly, with clear skies and open spaces. That settles it: I'm going to take a trip to Wordsworth country.

Chapter 4
Lost and Found

On Monday, October 26, I board a late-morning train to the Lake District. Once we're out of Oxford and its surrounding towns, the land turns into lush, green rolling hills dotted with Norman churches, manor houses, and the occasional inn or hotel. Here and there, small stone villages rise up out of valleys along the River Isis. After an hour gazing at "this other Eden," I make my way to the cafeteria car to purchase some lunch and return to my seat.

Finishing my pickle and cheese sandwich, I doze for a while and wake to the sound of the conductor's voice: "Calling at Staverley, Ings, and Windermere. Last stop, Windermere."

Windermere! That's my stop. I'm almost in Wordsworth country! At the train station, a tiny shed of a place, I alight and collect my case from the porter, who points me toward a taxi queue. The driver takes me a short way to my small hotel.

As I walk up the rose-lined path to the yellow front door of the inn, a short, elderly man with wiry gray hair and deep-blue eyes pops out and extends his hand to me. "Welcome! Welcome! Give me your case and come ye in, come ye in," he says in a froglike voice as he leads me inside. The small reception room has one tiny window, but the space is bright with vases of flowers and colorful pictures of lakes and mountains hanging on the walls. The innkeeper puts down my case, gestures to a pink velvet chair, and says, "Do sit down, ye must be tired from your travels." My chair is definitely vintage nineteenth century but clean and comfortable.

The innkeeper walks behind a tiny antique desk and flips through some pages in a book.

"Miss Kennard?" he asks, without looking up.

I stand up. "Yes, that's right." The innkeeper glances at me over his round, wire-rimmed glasses and smiles. "I'll show you to your room," he says, as he picks up my case and trots up an old mahogany staircase. At the top of the stairs, he leads the way down a long, green-carpeted hallway, hung with more pictures of lakes and mountains, and to a room at the end of the hallway with a private bath next to it. "No one else has a key to this loo, so don't worry about anyone else using it!" he says, perhaps in response to my surprised expression that the loo is outside my bedroom. "Well, I'll leave you to it," he says. He sets down my case and hands me two keys on a leather string.

I open the door and peek into a small room with a twin bed, a comfy rocking chair, and a Victorian wardrobe. Cream-colored wallpaper scattered with tiny pink roses covers the walls. Next to the rocker, a wide window looks out on gardens of more pink roses and boxwood. Behind this array of pink and green, three small lakes glisten in front of mountains stacked one upon the other as far as the eye can see.

After unpacking, I repair to the inn's lounge, where I find tea, delicious cheese scones, and a fire in the fireplace. An array of pamphlets laid out on a coffee table boast of endless adventure in the Lake District. One brochure about its many scenic trails intrigues me. After a dinner of toad in the hole, a dish of sausages in Yorkshire pudding with gravy and vegetables, I retreat to my room to read some Wordsworth and investigate which trail I will explore tomorrow.

The next morning presents gorgeous weather, cool but sunny. Time to explore the hills of Cumbria. I dress in wool pants, a wool sweater, my recent purchase of a pair of green wellies, a hat, and my rain jacket, just in case. I check with the innkeeper about the trail I want to walk.

"Aye, well, ye best be takin' a walkin' stick wich ya. It's a right steep one, that trail. Mind ye stay on the paths and cross styes with care," he warns, as he hands me a gnarled walking stick and a map.

"Thank you. I will be very careful."

From the inn, I walk up the narrow, tree-lined lane and discover the beginning of a trail marked by a stye, a tall gate I have to climb over unless I want to swing it open and traipse through mud and cow dung. The well-worn path is easy to follow and not as steep a climb as the innkeeper suggested. Soon I am deep in the Cumbria countryside, surrounded by haystacks, trees, and mountains. I climb with my walking stick, resting on styes as I go. At one particular place, the view brings to mind what the English poet Gerard Manley Hopkins calls "the dearest freshness deep down things."

Resting on a stye, I breathe in this world of undulating fields reaching up to blue skies. It's a blessing to be here. Thanks be to God for my courage to take this trip, one that puts me all alone in a part of England I do not know, something I've wanted for myself since I found out I'd be on exchange. It's also a chance to test myself to see if I've let go of some of my own sense of superiority. After all, anything can happen when one travels. If something unexpected comes up, will I be flexible or will I try to control things? Will I accept what I can't change and enjoy the time here, even if it doesn't turn out perfectly?

My hunger jolts me out of my reverie. I look at my watch. Yikes! It's now eleven o'clock, and I realize I have brought neither food nor water with me. I hope the breakfast I had at nine—eggs with tomatoes and mushrooms, along with orange juice, bacon, toast, and tea—will keep me going. I'm sure I can get some water at the pub noted on my map, and head in that direction. Though I'm off the trail, I can see the pub in the distance. It's a straight shot.

I walk a few yards in the direction of the pub. I turn to look back at the last stye I crossed. But it's not there. *What the heck happened to the stye? It can't have just disappeared.* I look for the pub, but now I can't see it. *This is too weird. Am I in some kind of sci-fi moment?* I shout, "Where's the bloody pub? Where's the stye?" Again, I look in the direction of where I last saw the pub and the stye and see only dark clouds swirling down toward me. *This isn't weird anymore; it's horrifying. I have no idea where I am, and I'm surrounded by these angry clouds.* Suddenly, there's an eerie moment of silence and everything feels stiller than still.

Then the sky opens and water like I've never seen cascades down. I don't know which way to go, but that hardly matters, since I can't see anything except water water water everywhere. It feels biblical, but where's the ark? I talk to myself again: "Don't panic. Keep walking as best you can in the direction you were headed before the rain came." So I hike, grateful for my hickory walking stick, lifting my aching legs out of the tall, wet grass, hoping I don't get stuck in the mud. Then a miracle happens. Aside from the rain, I hear another sound in the distance. I stop and try to listen. It sounds like humming. Could it be a machine of some kind? I try to walk toward it, but I'm wet through and through and shaking from the cold. The rain lessens, and another stye emerges. I run toward it and fall headlong into a mixture of mud and cow poop.

Look at me. I'm a mess. My clothes are wet and gross. What was I thinking, coming out here all alone?

Barbara, you can't do anything about your clothes. You have more important things to do. Get up and keep moving toward that sound you hear.

I stand up and try to brush off some of the goop on my pants. Grabbing my stick, I make my way to the stye and climb over it into more fields. There is no obvious path. The humming sound is still audible, and it's still raining. I walk and walk and walk until I come to another stye and cross it. This time, I use my stick to help me over it. I don't fall. The humming sound is still with me. Then, as suddenly as the rain arrived a few minutes ago, it ceases in an instant and the sun emerges. Within minutes, I'm hot and sweaty in my wet wool clothes. I strip off a few more layers and look around me. Behold! A herd of cattle lumbers across the fields toward a farmhouse. Cows lowing! That was the humming sound I heard. What a joyful noise. I never thought cows were so wonderful till now.

I follow them to the farmhouse and knock on the door with my stick. It opens. A bent old man with a beard and long gray hair stares at me.

Wagging his finger at me, he croaks, "I see ye comin' over the fields and was about to fetch ye. I figure ye come from the inn up the way? We always gettin' folks lost up here from the inn. Come in and sit yeself down by the fire. Take off them there boots and wet things. I'll fix ye a cuppa." The man puts a steaming cup of black tea with milk and sugar and a tin plate of crusty scones in front of me. I try to eat and drink neatly, but he barks, "Don't ye be standing on no ceremony for me. Finish up, and I'll take ye back to the inn."

After I gobble down the tea and scones, the farmer helps me into his truck, and soon we clank into the inn's driveway. I look out the truck window to the inn's garden. I think, *Blimey, there's no rain here. It's as dry as a desert.*

My innkeeper straightens up from his gardening and looks at me as I alight from the truck. Throwing up his hands, he shouts, "Ye look a right sight! Ye is covered in mud. What have ye done, ye daft woman?"

As the farmer drives off, I explain, "I got lost when it started to rain, but that kind farmer gave me tea and food and brought me back here in his truck."

"Aye, that'd be John Polemaker. He's always finding waifs and strays in his fields. Well, get yourself in a hot bath. It'll keep you from getting the chills." He then hands me a packet of eucalyptus-scented Epsom salts.

For an hour, I soak in delicious hot water. Then, once I'm tucked warmly in bed, it comes to me hard and fast how foolish I was today. I went on that hike without food and water, and, even more to the point, I should have reviewed the map with the innkeeper so I had a better sense of where I was going. It might have helped to ask about the weather too. I've lived in England for only a couple of months, but that's long enough to know that the weather here changes on a dime.

Tossing and turning in bed, I talk to the Almighty. "I'm thankful beyond words that I found mooing cows and a farmer. It could have rained all afternoon. I could have become utterly lost. I could have fallen and hurt myself. But I didn't, and I didn't try to control the situation or get upset because this wasn't a perfect hike. Indeed, I couldn't control anything."

I reach for a tissue and dry my eyes. Lying still, I remember the time I prayed after going to Evensong with Jacqui. In the storm today and in Christ Church Cathedral, I sensed a presence, that God was with me, listening to me. Now I want to talk to God more often. Handing over my worries and gratitude, I recall the opening verses of Psalm 31: "Into your hands, O Lord, I commend my spirit, for you have redeemed me, O God of truth." Instead of turning and tossing now, I want to commend my thanks to God for this day in the rain—indeed, for all of it: the lovely parts and the frightening parts. I pull up my comforter and curl up on my right side. Quietly I say, "Spirit of God, that farmer and those cows were no coincidences, nor was I just lucky. Your divine intervention was at work out there. I don't understand it, but I believe it with all my heart."

Lying on my back, I watch the evening light darken and turn on my night-table lamp. I reach for a magazine to read, but I soon put it down as more thoughts about my storm experience swirl in my mind. That storm reminds me of times in the past when I was in great danger but was rescued by some kind of force that I now recognize as God. This sense of imminent danger recalls again for me Gerard Manley Hopkins's poem "God's Grandeur," in which he explores humankind's powerlessness in the face of nature's cosmic energy. This experience in the rain reveals to me that yes, I can be strong and independent. I can be successful and accomplished, but I can never be like God; indeed, to strive for that is an act of idolatry, for only God is perfect. Yet for forty-five years I've tried to make everything perfect. Yet isn't it true that any given aspect of our human nature can be both a weakness and a strength? Sometimes we need to grab onto that thing in us that isn't usually a positive part of us. Had I not taken some control and instead given up during that storm, I might not be here now. Still, it's liberating to know I'm becoming someone who accepts that even my best will be fraught with flaws.

Returning from my Lake District adventures, I spend time with friends; we share meals and visit some of Oxford's museums and art galleries. I resume my walks around Port Meadow and the city center. At Blackwell's bookshop, some of the booksellers, who know me by name, speak to me. The lady who always serves me tea at the Queen's

Lane Coffee House asks me about my holiday. I tell her about getting lost in the fields. "Bloody hell!" she quips. "That was a near miss!"

Time has worked swiftly on me. Now, I don't mind some of the more annoying traits of the English that bothered me in September, the worst being the long queues at ATMs, grocery stores, or bus stops. Waiting half an hour for things that take only a few minutes in the States is just how it is here, and I'm glad to accept these quirks of English life.

I'm also not bothered when a friend or colleague teases me. Walking home from school shortly after my Lake District caper, I hear a Dragon teacher call out, "Hey, Ma Kennard. You look like you belong in Red Square with your big black coat, that black hat, and those black boots you're wearing." I look up to see him waving and grinning at me from a school bus loaded with Dragon kids. I could think, *How unprofessional of him to speak that way in front of students. They might get the idea they can talk that way to me, and I've already had a turd put on my chair—I don't need kids to start teasing me about my clothing.* But this is British humor and basically done in good fun. This is the way the English interact with one another. Perhaps it's even a compliment that my colleague jokes with me in the same way he would with a fellow Brit. So I smile and wave at him. A few days later, he strikes up a gracious conversation with me and, in a very different vein, asks how I'm getting along at the school. Am I getting out and about in Oxford? Do I ever get to London? Neither of us mentions his bus caper.

It's mid-November. Yellow leaves still fall from maples all over campus. I've been too busy to notice that Thanksgiving is coming up, and it dawns on me, *I'll be alone on Thanksgiving Day. I've never been alone on this holiday.* I'm not sure which makes me sadder, the fact that I'll be on my own on Thanksgiving or that there are no signs of the usual hoopla, such as Black Friday and American football,

associated with this holiday. I try to console myself with the realization that I'll be teaching all day, but the days leading up to the week
of Thanksgiving are horrible. I don't enjoy my work; I have sleepless
nights and feel a cold coming on. I'm also envious that Brady will be
headed to Dallas to be with his family for the holiday. During our
usual Sunday-afternoon phone date, he tries to cheer me up.

"Bear, I miss you so much."

"I miss you too, but I'll be there in about four weeks."

"My calendar's a mess with all the days crossed off already, but I'm
anxious about being alone on Thanksgiving. What am I gonna do
all day?"

"Could you eat with Jacqui? She must have had some Thanksgiving
meals while she was living in the States."

"She's gone to Cornwall to see her brother."

"Hmm, what about asking some Dragon people over for a potluck?
You're a great cook; you wouldn't have to make a big meal—just
something that would remind you of Thanksgiving, like your awe-
some pecan pie or your sweet-potato dish."

"I appreciate your ideas, Bear, but we will have been in school all
day, and most of my colleagues have kids and spouses to get home to."

"Oh, right! I forgot that you'll be teaching all day! But maybe that
will help you feel less anxious about not having a plan like you would
if you were in Boston. It may not be as much fun, but you could create
a meal of your favorite foods and find some music you like on the
BBC radio channels you listen to. Barb, you know how to take care of
yourself in situations like this. I think you can do that, and remember, it's only that one evening you'll be on your own. You'll be back
in school on Friday."

"You're right. It's kind of a blessing that I have school on
Thanksgiving, and I do like to cook, even for myself."

"I'm proud of you, Bearess. You're a strong, courageous woman. And remember, I'll call you Thanksgiving night at nine o'clock your time."

When I'm alone in my flat that evening, Brady's encouraging words remind me of Julian of Norwich's prayer "All shall be well, and all manner of thing shall be well." I go into my bedroom, light the little lamp on my table, and kneel down to pray. Waiting for words to offer God, I remain in that position. I don't seem to have any words, but the silence comforts me. Maybe God doesn't always need words. Then I tell myself, *I will make the best of being alone on Thanksgiving.*

Today is Wednesday, the day before Thanksgiving, and soon just about every American will wake up and begin preparing for the big feast. Schools will close at noon, the grocery stores will be crowded, the highways jammed. Yet in the midst of this reverie, I realize that I don't have to deal with any of these annoying aspects of Thanksgiving. I may not have family silver to use or a table to set, but I can buy a chicken or some ham and make myself a nice meal.

After my last class, I put my room in order and walk through campus toward the school gate. It's a sunny, windy day. I playfully kick golden leaves like I would if I were in Boston as I walk through the recess yard, enjoying the crunch under my boots. At the gate, I see Jenny and two other teachers: Betsy, who teaches Latin, and Debbie, a "maths" teacher. On occasion, the four of us have had tea in the common room together, but I don't see Betsy and Debbie much because we have very different schedules.

Jenny steps away from Betsy and Debbie, who are with some younger children, and strides toward me, brushing her dark-blond hair away from her face. "Hi, Barbara!" she calls. "I was thinking about you last night. I imagine it will feel a bit odd being in school tomorrow. Isn't tomorrow Thanksgiving Day in the US?" she asks.

"Well, yes. It's the biggest holiday in the States, but it's only one day. I plan to make a nice dinner for myself," I tell her.

Jenny buttons her coat as the wind picks up. "Why not come over for dinner tomorrow night? I'll invite Betsy and Debbie to join us," she says, as she nods in their direction.

I glance at Debbie and Betsy and smile. They smile and wave back as they walk back toward the tin can. "Gosh, that's so kind of you. I'd love to come, and it will be great to get to know Debbie and Betsy better."

"Brilliant! It'll be jolly good fun. I live about a fifteen-minute walk from Hernes Road. Shall we say seven p.m.?"

I consider the time of Jenny's invitation and the fact that Brady will call me later that same evening, then add, "Yes, but will it be okay if I leave in time to get back home by nine? My husband, Brady, is supposed to call me from Dallas, where he's visiting his family."

"Of course!" she says.

"Thank you, Jenny. See you tomorrow night." We both walk through the school gate, I to the left, she to the right, as we go our separate ways in the late-November afternoon light. It feels funny not to say goodbye again, as if I don't want this little meeting to end. I look in Jenny's direction to see if she might turn back to speak to me one more time, but she doesn't and I realize this is one more instance of the English way of "getting on with it"—a recognition that something is finished and it's time to do something new. It's so easy to hang on to something, when in fact it's better for us to let it go, to recognize that it's finished and that we need to move on to the next thing, however unknown it may be.

I adjust my rucksack across my back and head down Bardwell

Road, passing several boardinghouses. Their lights flick on as the sun continues to set. Some of the children play; others do their prep or "lay" tables for supper. A warm and homey moment fills me with a quiet peace. I say a short prayer of thanksgiving for Jenny's invitation, for this school community, and for the courage to "get on with it" as I continue down the road to catch the number 7 bus back to my flat.

It's Thursday, November 26. "Happy Thanksgiving, Barbara!" some teachers say to me as we leave morning assembly. In class a student asks me, "Ma Kennard, what would you be doing if you were at home today?"

Jack's question could make me sad, but he asks with a childlike wonder that reminds me how much God desires us to give thanks for all things. "If I were home today, I would get up very early, stuff the turkey, put it in the oven, and set the table with our family china and silver. My husband would lay a fire in our big stone fireplace and rearrange the furniture to make room for all the guests: my parents and my brother and his family. I always do the turkey, and everyone else brings salad, vegetables, or dessert. We have a tradition in my family that you bring the same thing each year. We all get very attached to my mom's apple pie and my brother's baked squash. So woe betide those who decide to bring something new to the meal!" I explain with delight and without the sadness I felt a few days ago.

Jack's eyes light up. "We bring the same things to our Christmas feast each year. That's so cool that you do that too."

Later that day, when I arrive at Jenny's tiny flat in a large Victorian house, I admire the small, round kitchen table set with an orange-and-yellow paper tablecloth and matching napkins. A vase of yellow and red flowers sits in the center of the table. Petite orange place cards have our names written in calligraphy. Debbie opens the wine I bring and pours a glass for each of us. Then Jenny raises her glass and gives a toast. "To Barbara: Happy Thanksgiving." Debbie and Betsy join in.

A few days ago, I couldn't have imagined that Thanksgiving would turn out like this. I manage to say, "And to all of you, thank you," I reply, as I raise my glass. I want to go on about how much I appreciate their kindness, about how a few days ago I thought Thanksgiving would be a washout and how they have rescued me. But I don't. I've learned that thanking an English person with simple words is enough.

"Cheers! Let's eat. Please sit down," Jenny says, as she brings food to the table.

"Jenny, what a beautiful table you've set. It looks very much like Thanksgiving to me," I say.

"Oh, I am glad, though I have to apologize. The market didn't have any cranberry sauce or any turkeys, so we have roast chicken and cranberry jam. I hope that's okay."

"It's brilliant! I've never had cranberry jam, but I'm sure I'll love it."

As we eat and converse about our lives, something occurs to me: I haven't thought about how I'm coming across to these women, nor about what I'm missing back home. I've known Jenny for a few months, and Debbie and Betsy even less time, yet they remind me of some of my oldest friends and how we pass our time together with ease and delight.

"Barbara, do tell us, how are you finding the Dragon?" Debbie asks.

Before I can respond, Betsy adds, "Don't hold back. Be honest! The Dragon has not had an opportunity to do an exchange with an American school in a long time, so we're curious to know what we can learn about our school from someone who teaches in the States."

"Gosh, I don't know where to begin. I'll admit I was shocked when I heard some of the teachers tell kids to 'shut up'! Dragon kids can be a bit rowdier that what we tolerate at Fessenden, but I still can't bring myself to say 'shut up' to my classes; that could get a teacher in real trouble in the States!" My admission leads to laughter all around the table.

After we collect ourselves, Debbie asks a more serious question: "Are you coping all right with the size of 'streams' at Dragon? I ask because sometimes I feel a bit overwhelmed by so many children at once!"

"Truth be told, I'm still adjusting to having twenty-five kids in a class, compared to the fifteen I'd have in a section at Fessenden. But I delight in the Dragon's marking system. It's very new to me, but so refreshing."

Jenny cocks her head to one side. "Really? How so?"

I explain how American schools and the Dragon use letter grades differently. In the States, an A indicates that a student has achieved the highest result possible, one that implies perfection. Moreover, American children don't have the option of moving to a higher section during the school year. At the Dragon, an A simply indicates that a student's effort falls in the top quarter of a stream; a child can have errors on work that still merits being in that top section. And if a Dragon student improves his work, he may be moved to a higher stream during the school year.

I also add my observation that the Dragon tolerates more naughtiness in kids than American schools. There, teachers are expected to deal with many issues of student behavior, regardless of how much time it takes away from teaching the rest of the class. I conclude, "Here, it's not a teacher's job to deal with every single aspect of a child's personality, as I would have to at Fessenden."

Jenny arches an eyebrow at my comparison of the two schools, "Well, yes indeed! We are here to teach and help kids. But we also expect children to take responsibility for their own learning. If they muck about and don't do their best, it's really all down to them." Then she suggests we all move into her lounge for coffee.

Soft orange-and-cream walls give light and warmth to the room on this cold November night. Off to one side, a space is filled with bookshelves and a large oak desk scattered with colored pencils, lesson plan books, and other teacher-y stuff. The three of us sit on two small sofas across from one another, with an oval, glass-topped table between us. I look out the windows to watch the evening darken, still surprised at how much later the sun sets in Oxford, but we are 450 miles closer to the North Pole than Boston is.

Jenny comes in with a tray and sets it on a tea cart nearby. Apologetically, she offers me coffee and a tiny cherry tart. "I am sorry, Barbara, but I couldn't find any pumpkin or apple pie. I hope these will do."

"They will do very nicely. You have been so thoughtful to try to create a traditional meal for me. Tonight has been a real Thanksgiving for me. I am so thankful for everyone's company and for the delicious food." Again, I stop short of lavishing too much American praise on my three friends.

They ask me how I'm getting on in Oxford, and I share my ventures to Port Meadow and the Covered Market. Debbie gives me her most recent copy of the *Oxford Times* so I can take advantage of the many plays, concerts, and art galleries in the city.

As much as I'm enjoying time with these women, it's starting to feel late and I'm anxious to get home for Brady's call. I look at my watch and make my excuses, "Oh, gosh! Look at the time. It's half eight. I'm sorry to have to go, but I'm expecting a call at nine from my husband, who's in Texas!"

"I have to go too," Betsy says, "and I can give you a lift back to your flat."

"Oh, thank you!" I put my coffee cup on the tray, stand up, and say, "Thank you all for this lovely evening. It has helped me to feel a lot less homesick."

Jenny hands me my coat and says, "It was a pleasure, Barbara! Why don't you take this jar of cranberry jam?"

"Thank you! What fun it will be to serve Brady some of it!"

At the bottom of the hedge-lined path leading from Jenny's flat, Betsy shows me to her dark green Fiat. I climb in. During the quick drive to my flat, Betsy tells me, "You seem to have fit in at the Dragon so well and so quickly. It isn't an easy place to be sometimes."

At first, I'm not sure if it's a good idea to share Upper 2B's turd prank; it happened a while ago, and I'm trying to live in the present. But Betsy has a sense of humor, so I tell her all the details.

"Blimey," she exclaims. "You handled that one with aplomb. Telling Upper 2B exactly how you felt in such a reserved manner will reap benefits for the rest of us teachers. In their eyes, you are now one of us," she says, pulling up to my building.

As I get out of her car, Betsy tells me, "It's been lovely to get to know you, Barbara. And by the way, all my friends call me Bets. Have a good phone call with your husband," she says, with a twinkle in her eye.

Unlocking the door to my flat, I hear the phone ringing. That's Brady!

I race to the phone, throwing my coat and bag on the sofa. "Hi, Bear! Happy Thanksgiving!"

"You too. You sound so happy. How was your day?"

"It was lovely. My mentor, Jenny, asked me for dinner and invited two other colleagues. We had chicken and cranberry jam."

"Cranberry jam? What's that?"

"You'll find out when you're here."

"Okay, you can surprise me with cranberry jam, and I'll surprise you with a few recipes I learned from one of the cooking shows on the Food Network," Brady says.

"What? You tried something new all by yourself? Who are you?" I joke.

"Just some weird guy you picked up at church ten years ago and asked out for brunch."

"Oh, that guy. He's a keeper."

"Good. You are too, and you have school tomorrow. Let's say good night."

After a bath, I climb into bed with the bear Brady put in my suitcase before I left Boston, but tonight I cuddle it without tears or anguish. I snuggle down and gaze around my bedroom at some pictures of my family and a print of the Oxford countryside that I bought at the Covered Market. I wonder if maybe this year won't be my only time in Oxford. Long before Brady and I decided to spend this year here, we spent a good deal of time in England as students and tourists, both together and on our own. During those years, we often wondered if we'd like to live here. Now we have that chance. Whether we return is uncertain but not impossible. Oh well—time will tell; it's all in God's hands anyway. I feel warmth flow through me. *What a blessing today has been.*

It's Tuesday, December 16, the first day of my monthlong Christmas holiday. Brady will be here in three days, and I've lots to do before he arrives. Jacqui lets me use her large washer-dryer combo. While my laundry is going, we have a light supper.

"Jacqui, you're very kind; I appreciate not having to make dinner."

"You must be thrilled that Brady is finally coming. When does he arrive?" Jacqui asks, as she ladles some minestrone soup into bowls.

I smile and say quietly, "Indeed I am."

Over supper, however, I also confide in Jacqui that I'm a bit anxious about how Brady will meet people without a work community like I have at the Dragon. I describe his dual nature: "Brady has a penchant for solitude, and he can also be very outgoing. I'll be at school Monday through Friday and on Saturday mornings. I worry that he'll be more content to sit in the flat, listening to music and reading, than getting out and about to meet people."

Jacqui reminds me of some things I haven't thought of. "I haven't met Brady yet, so I don't know him, but, given what you've told me about him and his performing around the world, I'm sure he'll make a life for himself here, even if he needs a little time to settle in. I shouldn't worry about him."

My heartbeat slows as I tell Jacqui, "I'm sure you're right. He'll be fine." We finish our meal, and I help her clear the table. As I take my leave, I say, "Thank you, Jacqui, for dinner and for your advice. I should probably get going and let you have the rest of the evening to yourself."

"Night-night, then, and here's your laundry!" she says with a grin.

Back in the flat, I fold my laundry. Soon I'll be folding Brady's too. At home I'd fold his T-shirts into triangles and pair up his socks into little balls of wool or cotton. But then he'd come along and toss them into his drawers any old way. I used to care that he made a mess of my handiwork, but he'd insist that he appreciated what I'd done. I'd come back with how much easier it'd be for him to find things in his drawers if he'd put them away carefully. Then Brady would take me in his arms and say, "You are *such* a fussbudget sometimes, but you're *my* fussbudget, and I wouldn't have it any other way."

Brady is very accepting of my quirks, but it probably doesn't help that he accepts my perfectionism. Recalling the sock scenario, I understand that my tendency to strive for the ideal, and my expectation of others to do the same, is about control. I want things done my way. But I also like folding Brady's laundry. There's something liberating about doing something for others just because we love them. It's when we want something in return for our gift that our support becomes something else, and we've lost our freedom to love as God loves us.

Laundry done, I flip through the arts section of the *Independent* newspaper and look for some things Brady and I might do in London. Too many options. I toss the paper on the floor and stare across the lounge at my big picture window. I walk over to it and look out. Nothing there of interest. Back to my chair. I pick up the paper and hunt for something again. But what? What am I looking for? My husband, from whom I've been parted for four months, is crossing the Atlantic in few days to join me. Isn't that more than enough? What else do I need? I glance around the flat and smile at the things I've added to it: plants here and there; a pretty pillow to soften the leather couch; knickknacks from Wordsworth country. Then I get it. When Brady arrives, what will happen to the life I've created here for myself? My independence? The freedom to do what I want when I want? And I wonder, *What do we do when we think someone we love might jeopardize our freedom?*

December 19, the day I've been waiting for since August 31, has finally arrived. Brady will be here by noon. Noon? Gosh, it's only 9:00 a.m. What to do? *I'll take a walk. That'll calm me down.* Strolling down the tree-lined path that connects my street to another one, I realize I've not thought about whether Brady's presence might hinder my independence. He's coming today, and that's what I want to focus on now.

Striding down Hernes Road, I play out a scenario in my head.

Brady might arrive early and call me, and I'll be out on this walk and won't know that he's called because the phone doesn't have an answering machine and what will he do?

I walk back to the flat, take off my hat and coat, and sit by the phone, but not for long. I get up and pace. Something tells me to sit down. I place my hands palms up on my thighs and close my eyes. I become aware of my breathing and remind myself, *Barbara, you've made it this far; you can wait just a little longer for Brady.*

At eleven thirty, it happens, and of course I'm in the loo when the phone rings. But I think, *This can't be Brady; it's too early. Maybe it's my hired car.* Hiking up my knickers, I race to the phone. "Hello?"

"Lovey, it's me! I'm here! I'm here in Oxford at the train station," Brady exclaims.

"Oh my gosh. You're early! I'll ring the car hire and get there as soon as I can," I say, and hang up. Never mind giving him a chance to say anything or realizing he could get a taxi at the station.

I ring the car hire. "Sorry, ma'am. Your reservation is for twelve. We don't have a cabby available now."

"But my husband is at the train station, and I've been waiting four months to see him."

"I'll see what I can do. Not promising anything, but be out on the pavement if someone comes."

At noon the car hire arrives, and we turn onto Banbury Road for the fifteen-minute journey to the train station, but cars and lorries line the road as far as the eye can see. Twenty-five minutes later, we round the corner at the Ashmolean and take the next left to the train station. Four or five cars queue for the entrance into the station. The driver pulls out of line and accelerates into the car park. But there's another line of cars. "Bloody England! Queues everywhere!" I mumble under my breath. The driver swings out and begins to circle around the car park, looking for a space. As we circle and circle and circle, I try to "keep a lid on it." As we go around one more time. I shriek, "Stop! There he is. He's at the top of the station stairs with his suitcases, in a cowboy jacket and boots."

"I can't stop here, ma'am! I have to park the car somewhere," my driver pronounces, as he continues to crawl around, looking for a space in the crowded car park.

I've waited long enough. Leaping out of the moving car, I call, "Brady!" and run toward him. He bolts down the stairs, leaving his cases behind. We land in each other's arms. A few minutes later, the driver is standing next to us with Brady's suitcases and my purse. "I think you both forgot something," he says with a chuckle.

Still arm in arm, Brady and I climb awkwardly into the backseat of the car as the driver puts Brady's cases in the boot. Once behind the wheel, he turns to us and asks, "Home?"

"Yes!" we chorus, as the driver zooms out of the car park and delivers us to our building.

Once inside, Brady looks around the front hall and the two bedrooms and exclaims, "It's just as you've described it to me; this guest bedroom really is tiny!" I show him into the lounge and the kitchen area. He takes it all in, sits on the blue leather sofa, and pats the space next to him, our signal to the other to come and sit too. We hold hands. He kisses me softly and says, "I like the flat very much, though I wish the guest bedroom wasn't so small. It would be better off as a small office or library where one of us could read if the other is watching TV or listening to music in the lounge, but otherwise it's very comfy. I like the plants you've added and the picture window. It reminds me so much of the flat I stayed in when I was a student at the Royal College of Music in 1969. It's small but has wonderful light coming through that big window."

A few minutes later, I suggest, "Let's put your cases in the guest bedroom and get some lunch in Summertown." After Brady unpacks a few essentials, we walk to Café Patisserie. As we stroll home after lunch, I point out several food shops, the bank, the chemist (pharmacy), and a few other places he needs to know about. Back in our flat, Brady takes a nap on our bed, and I try to read, but to no avail. I collect the morning post and actually wish I had some schoolwork to do. I try to read again but can't.

I put some scones in the oven to warm them and walk to the bedroom. *Snoring? Oh, right—Brady snores! Oh well. he can snore all he wants. I don't care one bit.* Funny how much that used to bother me. I yawn and lie down. Gently I massage Brady's neck and shoulders. He turns over onto his back and looks at me. We smile at each other; both of us get a little teary. He wraps his arms around me. We nuzzle like cats and hold each other in the afternoon quiet. *How many times did I lie in this bed alone, waiting for him? How often did I wrap myself in one of his sweaters or cuddle the bear he gave me? And now he's here in my arms. How wonderful.*

Soon, Brady whispers, "I am so, so happy to finally be with you again. I missed you so much, and I never want to be apart from you for this long again."

"Me too. Four months is a long time, but we made it!"

Chapter 5
Tough Love

January 1, 1999. The penultimate year of the century! During this last week of my Christmas holiday, Brady and I travel to London several times. We attend an RSC production of *The Tempest* and visit the Matisse exhibition at the Tate Modern.

After these adventures, we settle down to our routine of walking around Oxford, grocery shopping, and taking tea at 3:00 p.m. each day. We also go to Evensong with Jacqui and have her for supper after the service.

At Christ Church, we enter and find seats quickly, as the place is filling up. While the choir sings the opening canticle, the First Song of Isaiah, Brady watches them, his head tilted to one side, his left ankle resting on his right thigh, and his hands clasped loosely in his lap. I look at him, but his face focuses on the choir and I know this is not a time to touch him or take his hand. As the choir finishes, he turns to me and smiles. I smile back, and then we stand to sing the hymn "St. Clement." It's not familiar to either of us, but Brady sings it robustly. I try to follow him as best I can, since my sight-reading ability isn't anything like his.

Walking home after the service, the three of us fall into a pattern of two and one; at one point, Jacqui lets Brady and me walk and talk. As we pass shops and cafés, he points out the evening light on a stone facade. What a blessing it is to be married to someone who loves such things. Left on my own, I'd probably walk right on by and not notice the patterns of light. We take hands and cross the High Street. As we reach the other side, I ask, "Bear, what did you think about the service at the cathedral?"

"Oh, I liked it very much. I really enjoyed hearing the choral singing of the canticle; it was much more inspiring than the singing of the psalm, because the setting for the canticle was more dynamic than that of the psalm."

I smile inwardly at his music lesson and say, "I'm sure you liked the cathedral space, given your knowledge of church architecture."

We look behind us to see Jacqui keeping her distance. Then Brady adds, "The cathedral throws me right into the middle of a kind of Christian historical reality. What I appreciate is that it was built over a period of time, starting with the Romanesque style, and later the Gothic was added. Because of the different architectural styles, the building is so much more alive; it's an icon of the past, the present, and the future all in one; it gives me hope for life with God on Earth and in eternity."

"I knew from watching you during the service that you were taking it all in, the music and the architecture, but I didn't know that the building made you feel so connected to God. It's so nice, eight years into our marriage, to learn new things about you."

Brady whispers, "I think the same about you and your desire to reinvent yourself at the Dragon."

We reach the corner of High Street and Banbury Road, when the light changes for us to cross. Jacqui's still a bit behind us, checking out a store window. I take Brady's hand as we cross and suggest, "I wonder what Evensong would be like at some of the other colleges. Would you like to go to one at Merton College?"

Brady's eyes light up. "That's the college where you took that poetry class in the summer of 1997, right?"

"It is. I never went to any services there, but I'm sure it has an Evensong service; all the colleges do. It's sort of an Oxford thing, according to Jacqui."

"Let's check it out."

"I'll find some info on services at other colleges; we can try them all!"

Brady nods in Jacqui's direction. As she catches up to us, he points to our bus stop and the three of us hustle over to get on the number 7 bus to Summertown.

Back at our building, Jacqui goes to her place to freshen up and comes to downstairs to our flat for supper an hour later. I welcome her. "Do come in and sit down. Brady's just fixing the salad, and we'll eat soon. Would you like a glass of wine?" I ask, as she sits in one of our blue leather chairs by the front window.

"Yes, that would be lovely. Red if you have it, but white will do," she says, with a light laugh.

I hand her a glass of pinot noir and sit across from her in the blue leather sofa by the kitchen doorway so I can help Brady.

"Jacqui, you look like a model in one of Matisse's paintings with your colorful orange-and-yellow jumper," I comment as I sip some chardonnay.

"Oh, I doubt he would've had me as a model. He liked younger women! By the way, how did you like the Tate exhibit?"

"Very much!" Brady says, as he comes in from the kitchen and places a blue ceramic bowl of salad on the table. "It's quite a large collection. I could only take in so much in one visit, so I'll have to go again soon."

How odd, I think. *We were at the exhibition for a whole day. He commented about it a lot but never said he wanted to go back.* I pass a plate of biscuits and cheese to Jacqui and go to the kitchen to serve up the beef stew, thinking about what I just heard. *Why am I bothered by Brady's desire to return to the exhibit? Well, first, because he didn't say anything about two of us going—although, as much as I like looking at art with him, I'm not as interested in the details as he is. If we were in Boston, I wouldn't care about his going off on his own, but we've been apart for such a long time. I wish he'd suggested that we both revisit the show.*

I hear Jacqui offer, "I was meant to go with a friend next Wednesday, but she can't make it, so I have an extra ticket. Would you like to go with me?"

"I'd like that very much," Brady says.

I return from the kitchen and place a tureen of stew and a basket of warm bread on the table. Brady pulls out a chair for Jacqui and seats her. I serve each of us a bowl of stew and sit across from Jacqui. Brady pours more wine for us and sits at the head of the table.

"That's settled, then. We can see the exhibit, have lunch, see more of it, and get back to Oxford by six thirty. Will that work for you?" Jacqui looks at both of us.

"Yes. I can't think why it wouldn't!" Brady quips.

I try to make eye contact with Brady, but he's looking at Jacqui, so I clear my throat to get his attention, but he's glued to her. He probably didn't pick up that Jacqui looked at both of us when she asked her question, as a way of including me in the discussion of their trip. Brady often misses these sorts of nuances. But this isn't the time to say anything to him in front of her.

We finish supper. The clock in the kitchen strikes half seven. I offer pudding (dessert). "Would anyone like an apple turnover from the patisserie, with coffee?"

"I love pudding, but I shouldn't," Jacqui says, patting her tummy. "Been putting on a bit 'round the middle. I'll just have a spot of coffee."

"I'll have a turnover and coffee," Brady says.

I carry the supper dishes into the kitchen, make coffee, and put a turnover on a plate for Brady. I'm about to take it in to him when I stop. *Damn it! Why am I doing all this work while Brady sits in the lounge with Jacqui? Why doesn't he help me, as he used to back home? If I made dinner, he'd set and clear the table, serve dessert, and make coffee. We'd do the dishes together. But now he's just yakking away with Jacqui about Matisse.*

The kettle blows. I make the coffee and carry it into the lounge. Jacqui is deep into it, "That's so interesting to learn about Cézanne's influence on Matisse, Brady. I'm looking forward to seeing the exhibition with you."

Brady stands up. *Oh, yay! He's going to help me by pouring the coffee*, I think, as I stop to let him take the tray, but he doesn't; he doesn't even see me standing there. He's already headed over the bookshelf on the other side of the lounge. He picks up a huge book and carries it back to our table. "Here's the exhibition catalog," he says, "and here's the section on Cézanne and some of the other artists who influenced Matisse,"

Plonk goes the coffee tray on our dinner table. The china coffeepot and creamer and sugar dishes rattle, and Jacqui looks at me. I smile and sit. *I've done enough; Brady can play mother and pour the coffee.*

Brady takes the hint. "Jacqui, cream? Sugar?"

"A little of both, please."

"Barb? What about you?" he asks, as he looks at me with puppy-dog eyes.

"Just cream," I answer, turning away from his gaze.

The room grows quiet as we sip our coffee and Jacqui and Brady look through the Matisse exhibition catalog. The clock strikes eight, and, as if on cue, Jacqui says, "Barbara and Brady, I'm so pleased you invited me for supper. It's nice to have this time to get to know Brady a little more. But I must let you have the rest of the evening to yourselves. Brady, we can speak later about the timing of our trip to London next Wednesday. I'll see myself out. Night-night, and thank you so much for the lovely evening."

I hand Jacqui her wool wrap as we walk to the door. Brady appears, and we say, "Good night, Jacqui," almost in unison. *That's nice. We used to say goodbye together whenever friends left our house in Boston.*

Brady and I walk back into the lounge area, where the chairs are back in place at the table and the vase of dried flowers returned to the center. In the kitchen, the dessert plates and coffee cups have been put in the dishwasher, and I realize that Brady did all that while I was saying good night to Jacqui. Brady doesn't always apologize with words for what he's done, but he makes amends with his actions.

In the lounge, Brady continues to read the Matisse catalog and I look at the newspaper. The clock strikes eight thirty, and I'm reminded how delicious it is to have the whole evening ahead of us at this hour. *So many nights have I sat here alone, content with my own company, reading, watching telly, taking a bath, and going to bed, sometimes as late as eleven o'clock but always waking rested at seven. Back in Boston, exhaustion from my thirteen-hour day and the long drive to and from Fessenden meant bed by eight.*

I glance over my paper and see that Brady too is relaxed and engaged with Matisse; seems a good idea to let a little more time go by before I bring up the conversation I hope we can have tonight.

But Brady says, "Lovey, I'm a bit tired. I think I'll take a shower and get in bed with a book. Are you coming too?"

I love that he asks if I'm coming to bed too. Back in Boston, we'd always ask each other that question when one of us went off to our room. But I want to have that talk.

I test the waters. "I'm not that tired yet, but I would like to talk with you about your plans to go to London with Jacqui next week. Could we do that before you go to bed?"

"Okay. Let me shower first; then we can talk." Brady kisses me and walks to the bathroom. I hear the shower turn on and read more of the paper. At nine o'clock, Brady emerges from the shower in his pajamas and blue fleece robe. He sits on the sofa and pats the seat next to him. "Come and sit here."

When I oblige, he says, "What's on your mind?"

"I'm upset that you made plans with Jacqui without checking with me."

"I see. I didn't think going to London with Jacqui was a problem. Why didn't you say something?"

"I didn't say anything because it wouldn't have been appropriate to talk about our personal needs in front of her. Jacqui's a friend, but she would have felt uncomfortable if we'd started working this out in her presence. Brits don't do that sort of thing."

"I assumed you'd be in school all day and that going to London wouldn't affect you."

Taking a deep breath, I get up and walk to the other side of the room to straighten the pillows on a chair and tell myself it won't help the situation if I start explaining how different my Dragon schedule is from Fessenden, where I had no evening duties or Saturday classes.

Then, as if reading my mind, he looks at me with his little-boy face and says, "I'm sorry I haven't remembered some of the details of your Dragon schedule, but, having been on my own for the past four months, I'm not used to checking in with you about my plans."

Back on the sofa with him, I admit, "I know, but I figured once you got here, we'd return to our usual ways together. I don't mind if you go to London with Jacqui or by yourself. I just think we should check in with each other about our plans, as we would have back home."

Brady plays air piano with his right hand, something he does when he's trying to find words to say something, then responds, "I think you *do* mind."

"Maybe." I swallow hard. "I'm so used to making decisions, making things work here, struggling through it all pretty much by myself. Now that you're here, I hope we'll be a team like we were back home."

Brady reminds me, "We *are* a team. We've always been a team. Look, I may not use the words you want to hear, but being without you for four months was no picnic. For a month after you left, I didn't get much sleep; I had trouble doing my teaching, and it was a real effort to play my piano. Around October, I realized I had to do something to pull myself together, so I reached out to friends and tried to eat better and exercise more. Soon I felt like I could make it to December."

I put my arm around him and say, "I guess I didn't think this exchange would affect you. I'm sorry you had such a hard time, but I wish you could have told me some of this one of those times we talked on the phone."

"I thought I did, but you tend to allow your experience to cloud your vision of others."

"What do you mean by that?"

"It means that if someone doesn't say what you want to hear, you have difficulty grasping the fact that someone might have the same experience as you; you tend to think your experience is specific to you. It's as if you don't want anyone else to share in your situation, but if my experience had been different from yours, you wouldn't have liked that either."

"But your experience *was* different from mine—that's my point. You were at home with your job, your friends, and a familiar house, and you even had Stanley with you. I came to a foreign country to teach in a school I know nothing about. I didn't know anyone here. I had to move here by myself and settle in by myself. For you to take off with Jacqui for the day without asking me if it might impact me in some way upsets me. It makes me feel like you don't appreciate what I've been through. You imply that you've had the same experience, but I don't see how that could be the case."

Brady gets up and walks over to the picture window. He parts the curtains and looks out into the night. I stay on the couch and pretend to look at a magazine. Then he turns to me and says, "I just told you about my experience. Look, I don't want to talk any more about this. I'm really tired, and I just want to go to bed."

"Can we talk more in the morning?" I ask.

Brady stands up. "I think we've talked enough."

"Perhaps, but I'm not ready for bed. I'm going to listen to some music on the BBC."

"Don't stay up too late," he says.

"Okay. Good night."

"Good night," he says, and closes the door as he leaves the lounge.

I search the BBC schedule in the newspaper for its classical-music hour coming up. *Fiddle. All the music is either Wagner or Mahler. Dreadful stuff to listen to right now.* I toss the pillows on the floor and curl up on the sofa to think.

I struggle with Brady's independence. I'm independent, but not when I feel vulnerable, and right now that's how I feel. He's just arrived but wants to go off on his own. Part of me feels threatened when Brady does this, especially when I want to be with him, and it reminds me of times gone by when friends or lovers stopped being friends or lovers because I was too dependent on them and tried to control our relationship. Brady has never done anything to suggest he would leave me, but he does assert his independence for his own sake and sometimes for mine. Very early in our marriage, he wanted to resume his worldwide concertizing. He'd just finished his doctorate and had the time to travel and perform. I didn't really want to go on tour with him, but being without him for three weeks would have been much worse, so I suggested that if he went in the summer, I could go too. His response was "The tour will be very intense and tiring; besides, this is a good opportunity for you to be more independent." His words hurt and I was sad, but while he was away, I began to see that he was trying to help me conquer my tendency to depend too much on him. I learned how to be without him then, and I've done a pretty good job of it here in England too. But old habits die hard, and I will need to be mindful of this one during our time here and, indeed, in the years to come. I can do it; after all, I've been on the other side of this situation with students who wouldn't do something on their own, but I'd insist they try, even if it meant they'd fail, in order to succeed later. We all have definitive moments when we recognize how tough love works; though it can be painful and even frightening, we need to be pushed outside ourselves to discover our best selves. Having someone who loves you enough to give you that crucial nudge can make all the difference.

Chapter 6
A Dragon Teacher Now

Classes are back in session for Easter term on January 11, 1999. A major goal for me now is to help two of my classes prepare for their exams in the spring.

My thirteen-year-olds, Upper 2B, will take the Common Entrance Exam (CEE) to determine which secondary school they will attend next year. M3B, my ten-year-olds, will take the National Curriculum Test (NCT) to assess their skills in math, reading, writing, and science. Student scores on the NCT are used to adapt the curriculum so children will improve their knowledge over the next two years in preparation for the CEE. Weekly practice for both must begin now and will continue until the tests in May. English students don't prepare for these tests as American kids do for the SAT, ACT, or the ISEE, by taking special classes or working with a tutor. Rather, the English system exposes students to a plethora of material and ongoing practice beginning at age nine, with the expectation that children will do their best on the exams based on their individual abilities and will attend a school appropriate to those competencies.

Since October, I've exposed the children to a wide range of material. Now I need to afford them the same experience with practice assessments by giving them a variety of mock tests once a week. As I don't want to blaze through the process, thinking I should figure all this out by myself, I ask Jenny for advice one afternoon when we're both in Gunga Din, doing some photocopying.

"You'll find masses of practice exams and information on scoring them in the staff library. All the CEE material is in one area, and the NCT in another. Use practice tests from a variety of years, as the real test will include questions from recent and older assessments. Make sure you score each test the same day the kids take one, and then go over only the mistakes they have in common as a class. And don't waste time with kids who muck about—you'll have enough to do marking all the tests and reviewing common errors," Jenny says.

"This is really helpful, but how do I help the kids who have a lot of errors? Shouldn't I meet with them individually to help them score higher with each practice?"

Jenny looks at me with a slightly amused expression and gently replies, "Barbara, you don't have time for that, and we aren't expecting all of them to get 100 percent anyway. You've got to keep teaching them new material, as well as prep them for the CEE. We hope, with lots of practice, which I'm sure you'll give them, they will do their best and score in a range that represents their ability. The kids who don't, usually have not done well all year or have not taken this practice seriously. Don't bother with reviewing individual errors; most kids improve over time, and that's the goal."

Walking back to my room through the empty schoolyard, I chuckle at my ideas of helping the kids attain a higher score and explaining all their errors. Implicit in Jenny's advice is the reality that the amount of knowledge students attain is more important than high scores. Students may know a good deal about something but not necessarily achieve high scores on a test. What seem to matter at the Dragon are knowledge and effort, not arbitrary things such as percentages or grades.

Does Jenny know how much of a perfectionist I can be? She's worked with me for four months now, so she must have some idea, but she is kind enough not to mention it, as some colleagues at Fessenden might have: "Oh, Barbara, you are too perfect sometimes!" Instead, Jenny's honest appraisal of what the kids and I need to do to be successful affirms for me that it's possible, indeed necessary, to have high standards without expecting every single child to reach them. I was shocked at first when she suggested I not "waste time with kids who muck about"; at most of the schools in which I've taught, I would've employed my mantra that if I want kids to work hard, I should work harder myself and they should mirror my efforts. Now, I see there were even times when, consciously or unconsciously, I thrived on expecting kids to enter into a contest with me to see who could raise the bar higher. Most of my students didn't respond to that, so it became just me raising the bar on them and myself. This revelation reveals a hard truth: I equate perfectionism with being tough, so I need to find a way to have high expectations without intimidating students, without coming across as someone who is happy only with expert results. Come to think of it, what exactly *is* the consummate outcome? How elusive that seems to me now. We all can work and rework something and never achieve fulfillment, but is that the point? Since I arrived here four months ago, I have begun to understand that what matters is how to approach work. Do we expect perfection from ourselves and others as a sign of skill and effort? Or could we hand over our insatiable need for recognition for something less tangible, something more mysterious—a quiet fulfillment of work well done, even, if you will, work done to the Glory of God? Work that fulfills us so deeply that we have no need for perfection or recognition. Such an accomplishment is something we can treasure in our hearts, never to be taken away from us.

After my meeting with Jenny, I locate the necessary materials.

Most of the kids take the test prep seriously; the few who don't, I leave to their own devices, hoping they'll get with the program on the next practice test. I'd be blasted for such behavior at Fessenden—really, at just about any American school. Nevertheless, I remember Jenny's advice and my determination to be a Dragon teacher.

My learning curve continues in a conference with the parents of a boy who finds the practice exams quite challenging.

"Hello, Mr. and Mrs. Williams. I understand you have some concerns about Ronald's exam prep." I don't recognize myself getting right to the point; at Fessenden we'd spend the first five or ten minutes talking about the weather.

"Ronald has shared his recent practice-test scores with us, and we are concerned about how poorly he is doing," Mrs. Williams explains.

In an effort to give up some of my perfectionism, I say, in the most convincing voice I can muster, "The tests are very challenging, but I shouldn't be too worried about his scores now. It's only January, and we'll be practicing each week until May. I'm sure he will improve over these next few months."

Mr. Williams responds, "Ma Kennard, it will not do to tell Ronald he needn't worry about his scores. It is because the tests are hard that he should work harder. We don't expect scores of 100 percent—Ronald isn't capable of that at this point—but he is capable of something higher than 60 percent. Don't be afraid to tell him this."

After the Williamses leave, I reflect on their words. They're right. That the exams are hard *is* beside the point, and I knew this before they finished speaking to me. My conversation with them took me back to when I taught kids with language-related learning disabilities. It would have been insulting for those children to hear what I just said to the Williamses. My special-needs students knew they needed to work harder than those without learning challenges.

The next day, I speak to the Williamses' son. "Ronald, this material is very challenging for you, so you will have to work harder at it. Right now, the effort you're putting in isn't enough. Your answers on the last test reveal that you don't know what is being asked. Try reading the questions before you read the narrative; that will indicate what to look for. And take time to review your work. You finished the last practice test early and didn't go back to check your answers. You're a capable boy. I think you will achieve a score that reflects your ability if you put in more effort."

"Right, Ma! I will." Ronald is so accepting of my words, it's as if he knows he needs to work harder. Had I spoken like this to a Fessy boy, the response could have ranged from mild disinterest to strong disagreement.

Ronald's scores did improve a bit with each practice test, and by April he was achieving scores in the high 60s and low 70s. I also understood that the Williamses, in expressing their wishes, had revealed their confidence in me to demand more from their son, even though they sensed it would be difficult for him and for me. They never openly suggested that I was being soft in my approach, but I could hear it between their words. They were right. I was soft because I was afraid to be tough, partly to avoid expectations of excellence and also because their direct approach intimidated me a bit. In their direct but polite manner, the Williamses revealed an important truth: We cannot evolve in our work or in our personal lives if we don't recognize moments when we must change, try something different, even something scary, that will jolt us out of our usual practice. This is especially important if we are in any kind of leadership role where we model for others that transformative leap of faith.

In challenging Ronald, I decide this is good for the rest of the class. Soon I admonish them, "Upper 2B, it will not do for you to finish the practice test early and read a book. All of you will no doubt have some mistakes. Find them and revise."

Such absolute language is very different from "If you finish early, you can go back and check your answers," which is how I corrected American students. The latter is friendlier, but it implies a choice and doesn't communicate compelling expectations of excellence. Moreover, I've been listening to Dragon teachers speak sternly to students since September and notice that the children don't take such language personally; they take it seriously. In fact, they look for their teachers to speak this way. It's part of their culture.

In any event, it's a relief that exam preps are not required of my Upper 5 twelve-year-olds at this time. They light up when I suggest something they've been wanting to do. "Upper 5, why not take a break from the writing you've been working on? Sam, you had an idea to do a dramatization of something from *Slake's Limbo*. If you're up for it, today seems like a good time to do that."

For a moment, they aren't sure if I'm for real. Then Sam jumps up and takes center stage in front of my desk. "Right! Everyone stand up and count off by threes. I'll be the director, and we'll have eight groups of three."

Desks and chairs are rearranged; props are improvised from objects in the room: my hat for a turban, a jacket for a blanket, pads of paper for newspapers.

Don sits in the corner. "This is stupid. I'm not doing it."

Sam replies, "Yes, you are. You're with Johnny and Ben."

Don saunters toward his group, who grin and glare at him.

Gregor asks, "Ma, please, do you have any American money we can borrow for the scene where Slake resells old newspapers for his daily meal?"

By chance, I still have some stray nickels and dimes in my wallet.

Sitting in the back of the room, I watch this completely chaotic but wonderful improv come to life.

Jason, Bill, and Mike do a clever job performing the barter scene between Slake and "the man with the turban" for a newspaper. Sally, Angus, and Ned render a touching moment among the pink-faced cleaning lady, Slake, and a train worker as she reveals her fear of murder in the subway. Kindness comes across in Nigel, Dorothy, and Yiri's scene when two restaurant owners offer Slake a job in exchange for a daily meal.

When the twelve thirty bell rings, my dragons blaze out of the room, shouting, "Thanks, Ma. Class was brilliant."

My room is a total wreck. Some of the desks and chairs are shoved into corners, others turned into a train for a subway scene. But no matter—I put the desks and chairs back into five rows of five, retrieve my hat from where it was a turban, and spy a neat stack of nickels sitting on my desk. What is it about this class that I love? On the one hand, they are loud and messy, but, just like this stack of nickels, they can be collected, and on top of it all, I love this class because they *are* messy and they don't always have to get it right. I didn't consciously leave them on their own and slip off to the back of the room; I suggested dramatizing part of *Slake's Limbo* because I wanted to follow through on my earlier promise to Sam, although I had no intention of letting the kids be in charge. That could have resulted in lots of chaos and very little accomplished, something my "take charge" side would have struggled against. However, when Sam jumped up and took the reins, I let him. Something in me must have felt it would be all right, that this is how things are done at the Dragon and that it's okay—in fact, better sometimes—to let the kids figure it out. So what if it's loud and messy! Their scenes illustrated their understanding of the characters and themes in the story, yet I didn't even ask them to do that. Okay, it was chaotic, but I rather enjoyed watching them and not being in charge. I came to the Dragon to give up some of my perfectionism. Today, I did that!

Don't we all need to let go sometimes? To make room for whatever part of our lives is aching to be set free? That's not to say we should never take control; it's about discerning how and when to do that. Things get messy when we give up some of our control, but even then we must listen and trust that we will intervene without resorting to old patterns of behavior. What is so beautiful is the "dance" that can ensue between us and those we control when we try to run the show.

It's late January 1999. One afternoon after classes are over, Debbie sees me walking across campus and says, "Barbara, are you going to the four o'clock staff tea? I'll walk with you."

As we cross Bardwell Road, a strong wind sweeps by. We button up our coats and walk in silence for a bit, breathing in the crisp air. "How were your holidays?" I ask, chuffed that I'm now using English more readily.

"Jolly good. We were at home. Lovely to have time to just be in Oxford. And how is Brady? You must be over the moon that he's finally come," Debbie suggests, with a gleam in her eye.

We approach Hathaway House, one of the girls' boardinghouses hosting this week's tea, and I say, "Indeed! We are very happy those four months of being apart are over," as I open the front door to a large, airy sitting room with mahogany tables and upholstered chairs. Fifteen or twenty staff members chat as they drink tea and nibble biscuits. This gathering is one of my favorite moments of each week. With the day students gone and the boarders having tea with their house parents, it's a chance for teachers to slow down and socialize a bit before heading home for the evening.

"Good! I'm glad he's here. In fact, why not come for dinner? Say Saturday, eight o'clock? I'd like you both to meet my husband, Brian." Debbie says, as she nibbles a chocolate biscuit.

"How kind of you. We'll look forward to that!" *Finally! I've been hoping we might get an invitation like this.*

Saturday night's weather is fine. All we need are light coats, so Brady and I head off to Debbie and Brian's house on Stanford Road in Summertown, a little more than a mile from our flat.

At dinner, the four of us sit around a small table covered with a green-and-blue linen tablecloth and set with matching napkins and china. The English love flowers, so we have brought a bouquet of tulips and lilies, which Debbie puts in a simple crystal vase and places in the center of the table.

During dinner, Debbie engages Brady in conversation. "I understand you are a musician."

"That's right. I'm a classical pianist, and I teach music at a college in Boston. I'm on sabbatical and hope to do some composing and learn new pieces to add to my concert repertoire," Brady adds.

Pouring more wine into our glasses, Brian asks, "Do you have a piano in your flat?"

Brady replies, "Unfortunately, we don't. Barbara asked if I could use a piano at the Dragon, but with so many students taking lessons each day, it doesn't seem possible."

Brian and Debbie look at each other as they drink from their water goblets. Then Brian says, "We have one; we'd be happy to let you come practice."

Debbie adds, "It's seldom played, so you'd be doing us a favor! We'll have it tuned for you."

"Really? That's most generous!" Brady says, almost dropping his fork.

Brian beams. "Brilliant! Then that's settled. We'll give you a key to the house, and you can come anytime you want during the day. Sometimes I might be here, but don't let that keep you away. I would love to hear you play!"

"Thank you!" Brady exclaims, and raises his glass of wine to say, in his newly acquired English lingo, "Debbie and Brian, to your very good health."

The evening with Debbie and Brian winds down, and the weather is still mild, so we decide to walk home.

As we often do when walking, especially at night, we stroll together in silence for a bit. As we approach the Woodstock Road, I take Brady's hand and he blows me a kiss. We keep walking to the corner of Squitchy Lane and Woodstock Road. There, we turn right onto Squitchy and head toward the Banbury Road. Brady releases my hand and puts his arm around me as he says, "I love this street. What a funny name for it! Very English." He points to a large rose garden in front of a stone cottage and asks, "Shall I pick a rose for you?"

"You're sweet, but I wouldn't do that. Someone in the house might see you." We keep moving. I point out an orange cat sitting on a brick wall. Brady slowly approaches it with his hand outstretched, but it leaps off the wall and hides under a bush. We look at each other and laugh. We don't even need to say how much that cat reminds us of Stanley, our orange cat back home. As we stroll arm in arm to the corner of Banbury and Hernes Road, I think about this evening with Debbie and Brian in light of the one with Jacqui when she and Brady decided to go to the Matisse exhibit together. We've put the latter one in the history book of our marriage. We make every effort not to revisit it but rather to be better partners because of it.

—

Though I still walk to and from school in the dark, teaching at the Dragon continues to feel light and easy. My students and I get on well; they know what I want, and I've learned how to communicate my expectations in the Dragon style: a clear and no-nonsense delivery with a bit of humor sprinkled in. "Right, Upper 5, it's nine o'clock. I'm expecting your jolliest effort on a three hundred–word essay by half nine. Give it a go."

I figure out the exam practice and scoring and accomplish most of my marking during the day so I can spend the evening with Brady, even if it means staying at school until four thirty. Occasionally we go out for dinner or attend a concert at the Sheldonian Theatre or a play at the Oxford Playhouse with some of my colleagues.

One afternoon in the first week of February, I arrive home to unexpected news from Brady.

"Hi, sweetie. So glad you're home. Come and have some tea. I have something exciting to tell you."

"Okay, let me take off my coat first."

Brady hangs my coat and purse in the hall closet and goes into the kitchen. Returning to the lounge, he hands me a cup of tea.

"What's your news?" I ask, as I settle into one of our leather chairs and kick off my shoes.

Brady sits across from me on our leather sofa. "While I was playing some Chopin at Brian's house this morning, I met a violinist friend of his who's part of the Holywell Chamber Music Ensemble in Oxford. She and Brian listened to me play for a while. You'll never believe what happened next! The violinist told me about her group's upcoming tour in Romania. Their pianist can't do the tour because of a sudden illness, so she asked if I would be interested in taking his place."

"Brady, that's incredible!" I put down my tea and join him on the sofa.

"I haven't played in Europe for a number of years, and never in Eastern Europe. I'm glad you're pleased, but I want to know how you feel about my going away after just arriving here," he says, as he puts his arm around me.

Giving him a kiss, I ease his mind: "I love that you asked me that—you're the best Bear. I'll be just fine. There's lots of school stuff to do, and I'll get together with friends if I feel at loose ends. This is a wonderful opportunity for you, and I want you to go without having any worries about me."

We stand up together, and he takes my hand. "Okay, then I'll call the violinist and set up a rehearsal with the rest of the group to see if we play well together. If it feels like a good fit all around, I'll join them on the tour."

A few days later, Brady returns from his rehearsal in the late afternoon and calls out from the front hall, "Lovey, where are you?"

I open the door to the lounge where I'm vacuuming. "What?" I call.

Brady walks down the hall to me. "Well, we had a rehearsal. We played some short pieces to warm up. At first it was slow going; it took us some time to get into the same groove musically. Then we started the Brahms First Piano Quartet. After we finished the first movement, which is really fast and very demanding on the pianist's right hand, the violinist stopped playing, so I was worried they didn't like my playing. You know how quickly I can sense with American musicians how things are going when we play together, but I never got that feeling with these musicians. So—"

"Brady! You're up to your old tricks of keeping me in suspense! Tell me!" I laugh and put down the hoover.

"So, the violinist said, 'We don't need to play anymore unless you want to. You are a consummate pianist, and we would be delighted to have you join us in Romania.'" He beams.

"I am so thrilled for you. Let's go to the Greek Taverna to celebrate. My treat," I say, and together we put on our coats and hats and set out on our walk to one of our favorite restaurants in Summertown.

The following week, Brady prepares to take the train to London to fly to Romania. Before I leave for school, we say goodbye. "I'm so excited for you, Bear. I know you'll enjoy every minute of this trip. You'll be in your element! Don't worry about me, but call me when you can."

"Bearess, you're the best! You understand how much music means to me, but it will never mean more to me than you do. Take care of yourself. I'll call when I get settled in Bucharest."

At four o'clock the next day, when all the kids are gone and only a few teachers remain on campus, I'm sitting in my classroom, thinking about what I want to do with my students for the next few weeks, when an unexpected feeling wells up in me. Brady called me very early this morning, but now I feel sad. What's that about? I'm in a much better place now than I was four months ago, but I still feel a bit empty. Is it because Brady is away? No, it doesn't feel like the sadness I felt in the autumn when I was here alone. It's something else, but what? I gaze around the room at all the wonderful student work I've posted on the walls, but the only answer I find is that I have work to do and can't let my melancholy get to me.

My students. What do they need? What do they love to do? What do I love to teach? With some ideas in mind, I take books and hand-made materials out of my closet and arrange them around the room to inspire me. It's almost March, and our monthlong Easter term break is coming in early April. M3B and Upper 2A must keep their noses to the grindstone and continue their exam prep for the tests in May. Lower 2A can finish their book reviews and practice diagramming sentences. Upper 5 could do something off the charts. Maybe Shakespeare.

April? May? Oh, I get it. My sadness has to do with these two months. April comes before May, and then there are June and July, and we have to go back to the States at the end of July. "I don't want to go back to the States and Fessenden!" I shout out loud, wondering if teachers in this tin can building can hear me. If I were back at Fessenden right now, I'd feel pressure from the kids and other teachers to loosen up a bit before spring break. "Do something fun; the kids are in vacation mode already, so you won't get much work out of them now," some of my Fessy colleagues would say, and I'd feel guilty if I didn't lower the bar and guilty if I did. But here at the Dragon, I can maintain expectations up until vacation, knowing that kids everywhere rise to whatever bar is set for them. And this time I can do that without being such a perfectionist, because it's okay at the Dragon to expect a lot from students. Come to think of it, lowering my expectations probably has led me to strive for perfection both from my students and from myself. Impeccability has thus become a substitute for high standards that are discouraged in American schools but, fortunately, that are the norm at the Dragon. As long as we work hard at hard stuff, we don't need to be perfect.

Walking home at the end of the school day, I recall my outburst in the tin can. I can't believe I did that. How un-English of me. Yet I feel so English because I fit here. Friends and colleagues here inspire me and don't make me feel like an outsider. People here are genuine with their thoughts and words. They aren't afraid to say what they think, but they do it so politely, you'd hardly know they were giving you advice or correcting your mistake. I can't imagine what it would be like to fit back into life in the States—driving everywhere; reentering a much faster pace of life; no tea at local boardinghouses. And Jacqui! I'd miss her so much. She's the first friend I've made here and is such a support to me. And how will I step back into teaching the Fessenden way? I love the way the kids and I work together here and the materials we use, especially that time Upper 2B did those amazing scenes with *Slake's Limbo*. I wanted to be one of them and let one of the kids be me.

Passing through Summertown, I'm almost home, so I strategize about how to tell Brady about my revelation in the tin can. He's been back from his concert tour less than a week, so I'll pay attention to his energy and notice when he's fully rested. Then I'll share my feelings over dinner at one of our favorite restaurants. I'll describe my realization that time is moving more quickly now; we've been here longer than the time we have left, and how I don't want to leave. I'm not sure how Brady will feel about this—we've never talked about not going back to Boston—but I want to share this with him because neither of us would try to deal with something this big on our own.

I open our flat door to hear music blaring from our little radio. As I hang up my coat and walk into the lounge, Mozart fades and Brady calls out, "Hi, lovey."

Oh, good. Sounds like he's got his usual energy back. Though I thought to share my feelings over dinner, this seems to be the better moment. I'll make us some tea and tell him.

As we sip Assam, Brady asks. "How was school today?"

What a great opener! I was afraid I'd have to bring up the subject, but he's done it for me.

"I'm glad you asked, because I have something I need to share with you." I sip more tea, glancing at him over my cup.

"Sounds serious. What's your mind?"

He's making this easy for me, but I don't think he has a clue what I'm about to say. I put down my teacup and take his hand, "Brady, I had a startling moment in my classroom today. When I was working on some lesson plans, I began to feel sad about the little bit of time we have left here. Without any warning whatsoever, I blurted out, 'I don't want to go back to the States or to Fessenden.'"

Brady assures me. "I understand that. I felt that way when I lived and studied here thirty years ago. I'll miss being here too. England is a special place to both of us for many reasons, but I'm sure we'll come back."

"I'm sure we will . . . or we could stay here," I offer.

"It'll be a real loss for us both to leave here. We've made such good friends, you've been so successful at the Dragon, and I've had musical opportunities that probably never would've happened in Boston. We could stay here, but it would entail so much upheaval in our lives. What would we do for income? What about our house in Quincy, and Stanley? We'd miss our friends and family. I can't see it."

I'm not surprised at my practical husband's reply. I pick up my teacup and turn away from him. Brady rubs my back. "Barb, let's enjoy the time we have left here and plan to come back. Maybe next summer. We'll stay in touch with our friends and be able to visit them when we return. We can come back to visit as often as we want. England will always be like a second home to us." He hands me a tissue.

I wipe my eyes, blow my nose, and say, "That sounds nice, but I really don't want to go back. I feel so much a part of the Dragon community in ways that I'll never experience at Fessenden."

Brady takes a deep breath and looks away from me for a second. "You don't know that for certain, especially since you came here to learn how to become the teacher you want to be. Won't you miss seeing how this plays out at Fessenden? You won't have that opportunity if you stay here. If for no other reason, you owe it to yourself to see how this all comes to fruition back home."

I run my fingers around the rim of my cup and look at him. "I hear your points, but this revelation I've had feels too big and too important for me not to take the time to consider it more. I'm not ready to make a decision now. And I'd like some space to think more about it."

Brady drums his thumbs on his thigh and then takes the tea things into the kitchen. A few minutes later, he returns to the lounge and says, "Okay, Barb. I suppose if that's how you feel and is what you want, then that's what we'll do."

Chapter 7
Difficult Choices

March comes in, and the sun makes its first appearance in a while. I take my nine-year-olds to Lymans Hall for their drama class to create scenes from a new book they're all bonkers over, *Harry Potter and the Philosopher's Stone*. Playing Harry and Hermione propels Lower 2A into a marathon of running, screaming, and rolling about on the floor.

After I make several attempts to settle them down, they still can't focus. So I say it: "Lower 2A, stop! Sit down and shut up!" Twenty-two nine-year-olds plop down on the floor and smile because I've finally done something all Dragon teachers do: I've told them to shut up. Then I follow up with what seems like a helpful antidote for their restlessness.

"Right! Lower 2A, all of you, outside for two minutes. Run 'round the playground and get your willies out." I open the door.

A moment of really uncomfortable silence follows. The girls try to suppress their giggles, but the boys just stare at me in utter disbelief. I say it again: "Come on, you have too much energy. Run 'round the playground and get your willies out. Then we can have class."

The kids look like they've seen some kind of sci-fi thing. Looking at the girls' faces and the boys' body language, I suddenly get it. A horrible feeling deep in my gut tells me that I have said something really wrong. I know in that sickening instant that willies are not what they are in the States. Americans don't look horrified if someone says, "Oh, that horror film gave me the willies," or if someone describes excess energy as "the willies." But in England, willies are something else entirely. This is one instance where Americans and English people do not share a common language.

I plaster on my teacher face and exclaim, "Right! Lower 2A, I'm so sorry about my mistake with *that word*. You can come back inside."

The kids can't get back in Lymans Hall fast enough. There, more silence ensues, but I can't help laughing. "Lower 2A, I think I just gave you an example of how some words in the US don't have the same meaning in England! In the States, the word I used—I won't say it again—can mean that you have too much energy. I wanted you to get rid of your excess energy so you could focus on your *Harry Potter* scenes."

"That's okay, Ma!" they exclaim. Relief echoes around the hall. I take their cue, and we move on to their Harry and Hermione skits. Their gleeful performances make me laugh, but as class comes to an end, I wonder, *Will my mistake have repercussions with parents and the administration?*

At bun break, I ask Jenny for a minute to talk with her.

"Of course! Shall we go to my room?"

Once Jenny has closed her classroom door, I relay the scene from my class. She roars with laughter, "Ooh! I bet that went down well with the troops. I assume you know now what willies are."

"Yes, I figured that out pretty quickly, based on the way the boys were looking at me. I tried to explain that words can have different meanings in different cultures. The kids took it pretty well."

"You made an honest mistake and handled it professionally. I shouldn't worry about it. Let's get a coffee in Gunga Din."

As we walk, I confess what I'm really worried about: "What if the students share this with their parents? Even if one of the kids thinks it's funny, a parent might get upset and call the head of school."

"Barbara, most of the children have probably forgotten about it, and even if they do tell their parents, I doubt very much their mums and dads will do anything other than laugh. You taught the kids a valuable lesson about language, and, most importantly, you acknowledged your mistake. That's a sign of strength."

The next day, Lower 2A's *Harry Potter* scenes cleverly demonstrate their understanding of the characters, conflicts, and themes of the book, and I grasp something else about these dragons and about myself. They were successful with their drama scenes because they didn't take my mistake personally, and I didn't fixate on my blunder and try to make the situation A-okay. The English expect only one admission of a mistake, so I knew not to mention my faux pas again, though at first that omission felt a bit odd. In the past, I apologized over and over for the smallest misstep because I felt pressure from a school and from myself to get everything right. Once, when I forgot to return a parent's phone call, I heard the same response from the student's advisor, the dean, and my department head: "We all strive to return parent phone calls within twenty-four hours of when the call was made." But one apology wasn't enough for them. I had to say it to each person who called me out.

Throughout the rest of March, Lower 2A creates wonderful drama scenes from some of the books we read as a class: *The Horse and His Boy*, *Skellig*, and *Tom's Midnight Garden*. And nothing more comes from my "willies" moment; I receive no parent phone calls, no questions from the administration, no comments from other students. If students, staff, or parents know about it, they say nothing to me, nor do I detect conversation about it. It was as if it had never happened. I recognize this silence as one more example of English courtesy. The students weren't embarrassed for themselves; if anything, they were embarrassed for me. But they would never reveal these feelings. The kindest thing they could do was not ever speak of it again. It's such a human thing to show sympathy toward someone who's made an awkward mistake. Is it possible that discretion *is* the better part of valor? Wouldn't it be more loving to withhold our comments and allow such situations to be resolved through our actions, rather than our words? Sometimes less really is more.

Brady and I travel to Dorset and Salisbury during Easter break. The afternoon of our return to Oxford, I sort through the post while he puts in a load of laundry. My eye catches a letter from Betsy. There's also a packet from Fessenden. I have no idea why Betsy would write to me, so I open her letter first.

Hi Barbara,

I've been trying to reach you, but perhaps you've not got an answering machine. There are going to be two English openings at the Dragon for next year. I doubt we'd find someone who has your breadth of experience with children of all ages, so it would be a waste of our time to look elsewhere for a candidate. I hope you will consider applying for either or both of these positions: teaching English "across ages," as you are doing this year, or teaching all the twelve-year-olds. As a senior member of the search committee, I have a voice in who we hire. Do let me know if you are interested when you return to school from

your holidays, and I'll speak to the deputy head on your behalf.
It would be jolly good to have you back next year!

   Enjoy your holiday.

   "Bets" Montgomery

My heart pounds. Maybe my tin can revelation was more than a revelation! I'm already picturing myself in a classroom here next year. My Upper 5 class is a dream to teach. They're so clever and so interested in learning. I adore their delightful mix of seriousness of purpose and fun. Then I realize that next year's Upper 5 are this year's M3B, so I'll know some of the kids. How cool is that! But the packet from Fessenden is staring me in the face. No doubt it's my contract for next year. I'll put it in the guest bedroom and look at it later, No, wait—that's not a good idea. I might forget about it. I have to face the music.

Dear Barbara,

   I hope you and Brady are doing well and that you've been enjoying your exchange year at the Dragon School.

   Enclosed you will find your contract and outline of duties for the 1999–2000 school year. I have not changed any of your assignments from the 1997–'98 school year, when you were last with us, but if you have any questions or wish to consider new responsibilities, I will be happy to meet with you anytime in August. In the meantime, please read through these papers, sign the contract page, and return it by May 15, 1999.

   I wish you a successful end to the school year and am eager to welcome you back to Fessy.

   Best wishes,

   Fred Post, Headmaster

Wow! A job at the Dragon looks like a real possibility, but this Fessenden contract feels real too. Fred's letter is so friendly, and he's giving me the chance to consider other options with my job.

Brady walks into the lounge and says, "What's up, lovey? You look perplexed."

"It's this packet from Fessenden and a letter from Bev about a job at the Dragon for next year." I hand him the letter.

"Well, Bets's letter is certainly a compliment to you, but you have a commitment to return to Fessenden."

Taking a seat at our dining table, I tell Brady, "Bets's letter reminds me of that moment I told you about when I realized how much I don't want to go back. This letter sounds like staying here is a real possibility, but Fred's letter clearly states they expect me to return."

Brady raises his eyebrows. "Of course, they expect you to come back."

"Yes, I know that." I toss the Fessenden packet on the table and go to the kitchen to make a snack.

Brady calls from the lounge, "If I were Fred, I'd be pretty upset if you told me you weren't returning."

I come back to the lounge and put a tray of cheese and biscuits and water on the table between us. "I suppose he could be, but I didn't sign anything that binds me to another year at Fessenden."

As we make ourselves cheese "sandwiches," Brady adds, "That's true—it's not as if they asked you to sign a contract for the 1999–2000 school year before you left. But it's clear they're taking your word that you'll be back."

Brady goes into the kitchen and turns off the dryer. Settling back in my chair with my cheese, I wonder, *What do promises say about us? If we honor them, we reveal our commitment, but if we break them, does that demonstrate selfishness? Sometimes promises can't be fulfilled, for reasons beyond our control. But what about those situations that are within our control, those times when we want to have our cake and eat it too? Do promises always bind us? Are there ways to back out of a promise without losing one's integrity?*

The dryer door bangs closed, followed by more silence from the kitchen. I call out, "But I never literally gave them my 'word.'"

My husband sticks his head around the corner and counters, "But does that mean it's okay for you to leave Fessenden in the lurch?"

"Brady, I want to talk more about Bets's letter and what this possibility could mean for me. It feels like you're more concerned about what it would mean for Fessenden if I were to stay here for another year."

Brady brings our clean laundry into the lounge and throws it in a nearby chair. "I'm concerned what this decision to stay at the Dragon might mean for you in a different sense."

"What are you saying?" I whirl a facecloth from the laundry pile at him.

Catching it, Brady speaks deliberately: "It's wrong not to return to Fessenden. Not because you didn't get the Winsor job, but because it's not who you are." Brady looks at me and reaches for some laundry to fold. We both fold for a minute. Then he adds, "You are a person of real integrity who goes out of her way to do the right thing." I look at him as if to say, *Don't remind me of my good points—it might make it easier for me to do the right thing and go home.* Laying on the guilt a bit thicker, Brady reminds me of my honest approach with Fessenden about why I needed this exchange. He reads my mind and adds, "Staying here could feel like a slap in the face to the school. I think you'd regret that in the long run."

"Maybe, but I also might regret it if I don't explore this opportunity. Besides, I don't have the job yet!" My stomach growls. I'm not sure which has made me hungrier, folding laundry or arguing with Brady. I plunk myself down in the chair by the window and consider the trials of making decisions together. In any committed relationship, two people depend on each other, but in a mysterious way our independence can draw us closer together as we seek advice, solace, or even constructive criticism we may need but don't want to hear. And the space that emerges between these dynamics can be a place where we find the courage to resolve difficult situations together.

Between bites of his cheese, Brady counters, "No, but it's a good chance you'll get it. It is almost as if the decision to hire you has already been made, but there's a bigger picture here, which I've tried to describe to you."

Taking his hand, I say, "I know, and even if I'm not in agreement with you, I appreciate your honesty and concern." I go on to describe how change is a common and accepted phenomenon in independent schools, and that Fessenden might well understand if I were to stay here because of the support it offered me with the Winsor job.

Brady pours himself a glass of water and drinks it all with that slow, deliberate motion I know well. He silently places his glass on the table and speaks his mind. "I understand what you're describing, but that doesn't necessarily make it right."

"You might think it's not right but working in independent schools is very different from teaching at the college level, where faculty have tenure, as you do. You can't be fired. But, in private schools like Fessenden, teachers are dispensable. Private schools don't have teacher unions to help them negotiate these situations—we have to look after ourselves. I think I can do that and still retain my integrity." I stand and carry the food tray back to the kitchen. Brady follows.

As we clean up, we agree to take a break and talk more later. Jacqui is coming for tea this afternoon, so we unpack from our trip and have a lie-down. An hour later, I am awakened by some rattling sounds and wander into the kitchen.

"Are you well rested?" Brady asks, and kisses me.

"I am! And this tea tray looks lovely with our white linen tea towel and the green china teacups we bought in Salisbury."

I put chocolate biscuits on a plate and some white linen napkins that match our tea towel on the tray.

Then I hear Jacqui knock on our door. "Come in, come in!" I usher her into our lounge.

"It's so good to see you. Do sit down. Brady is making tea."

Jacqui takes her favorite seat in our cozy blue leather chair by our dining table. "You've made a nice tea. Both of you are getting to be quite English with such a proper tea and use of our language. You'll just have to stay here in Oxford and not return to Boston!"

I exclaim, "Actually that might be a possibility. I just found out—"

Brady interjects, "We love Oxford, but we both have to go back to our jobs in Boston."

I can't believe my ears and spill tea all over the carpet and on Jacqui's shoes. "Oh, I'm sorry, Jacqui!" I say, trying to wipe up the tea with my napkin.

"No worries, Barbara. But you do look quite bothered. Did I say something to upset you?"

"No, no. Excuse me for a minute while I get something to clean up the rest of this mess. Do carry on with Brady." I walk to the kitchen and kick the door shut. *How could Brady jump in and tell Jacqui we're going back to the States? What is he thinking, especially since we've agreed to talk more about it? Does he think that by telling Jacqui we're returning to Boston, I'll give in to his way of thinking? No way!*

I grab a towel and return to the lounge. "Here we go." I press the towel on the carpet and Jacqui's shoe to mop up the rest of the tea.

A bit of silence ensues. Jacqui sips her tea and looks at a poster of London on the wall of our lounge. Brady looks at me and rolls his eyes; I shrug my shoulders because I don't know what to say, embarrassed that we both, in our own ways, have brought up what Jacqui would consider private business. I'm grateful when Brady starts a new conversation: "Jacqui, what's new at the Ashmolean Museum, and do you still like your part-time job there?"

"Oh, yes. I quite like it. I've just accepted a full-time position starting this summer. Speaking of summer, when is school over for you, Barbara, and when do you two plan to return to the States?"

I jump in: "School is over on July sixteenth, but I'm not sure I want to go back to the States. Oxford feels more like home to me now than Boston."

Brady stands and takes hold of the teapot. Gesturing to Jacqui, he steps toward her and asks, "More tea?"

"No, thank you, Brady." She turns towards me and asks, "Is there some way you could stay!"

"Well, there might be—"

Brady interjects, "No, Jacqui unfortunately, we can't stay. Barbara has an agreement with her school that she will return after the one-year exchange, and I have to go back to my college, since my sabbatical will be over at the end of this summer. We'll be headed back to the US on July 31." Brady puts down the teapot with a dull *thud* and sits in his chair.

Here he goes! Brady is speaking for me again! *What an HA* [horse's ass—our jibe for each other when one of us has done something asinine].

"Yes, quite! I would imagine that both your schools will want you back, and if you have an agreement to return, you will want to honor it. And the teacher taking your place will no doubt want to return to England," Jacqui suggests, with a bit of authority.

After some inane chitchat about the weather, Jacqui makes her excuses and exits. Brady and I carry the tea things into the kitchen. He washes, dries, and puts away the tea dishes and takes up his book in the lounge. I fold the rest of the laundry. I want to tell him how upset I am, but I don't, because his slow and deliberate manner with the dishes tells me he knows how I feel. My frustration is somewhat assuaged knowing that we still do what we've always done when we disagree: We remain in the same room or close by.

After some time together in silence, I say quietly, "I'm upset that you cut me off twice and told Jacqui we'd be returning to the States. We haven't made that decision yet; we agreed we would resume our conversation from this afternoon."

Brady puts down his book and folds his hands. "I jumped in because you started to tell Jacqui that we might stay here. I still feel the same way as I did when we talked earlier, but I'll hear what you have to say over dinner. Let's go out. Being in a neutral place might help us to listen better."

That evening, we walk to a favorite restaurant. Brady takes my hand as we cross the busy Banbury Road. We order our meals, and I launch in: "I would like to look into the position with the twelve-year-old age group at the Dragon when I get back to school. I'll get all the information about the job description, the salary, and the benefits and share that with you. If we think we can swing it financially, I'd like to apply for the position."

I also suggest that he ask for a year's leave of absence at ENC and look for a teaching position at the RCM (Royal College of Music) in London, where, as an honorary fellow, he'd be eligible for part-time employment.

Brady acknowledges these possibilities but reminds me there are more reasons we can't stay. I buy some time by excusing myself to go to the loo, even though I don't have to go. Inside the toilet, I exhale the tension I feel, splash some cold water on my face, and head back to the table.

"Okay," I say as I take my seat. "What are these reasons why we can't stay?"

"That was the shortest trip to the loo I've ever seen you take!"

I can't help but smile. "Very funny! To be honest, I needed to take a break before hearing what you have to say."

Brady relaxes his posture a bit and begins, "In addition to all the reasons I cited earlier today, there are some practicalities we haven't discussed."

Our server comes by to check on our meals. I ask him to bring more water, after which Brady and I chuckle; we still find it funny that they don't refill your glass automatically here. We each take a pleasurable gulp. There is more silence while we eat, and then Brady continues, "I can't take your idea seriously, because we've agreed we don't want to be apart for such a long time again, and that could happen if ENC doesn't give me a leave of absence or if I don't find a job here. Perhaps I should have made that point earlier. I focused on your integrity because it hurt me to think that you might be okay with our being apart again."

Choking on my chicken, I wash it down with a gulp of wine, followed by water. I've done it again. I've jumped into something without thinking it through, "I'm sorry, Brady. I hadn't thought of all these factors. Betsy's note was such a wonderful affirmation of my desire to stay here, but I never considered the possibility that we might have to live apart again. I don't want that!"

Brady takes my hand from across the table. "That's okay, lovey. I love the way you dream big. We wouldn't be here if you hadn't! I'm glad I can help you see the details you might miss, just like you help me to see the bigger picture I rarely notice."

I snuggle up to him in our booth and whisper, "You're the best. I love you. Going back to Fessenden isn't what I hoped for, but I do see the bigger picture. I'll sign the Fessenden contract and mail it back, and I'll find a way to tell Betsy I can't apply for the job when I get back to school."

Chapter 8
The Beginning of the End

It's May 16. Easter term break is over, and school is back in session for summer term. I walk everywhere now in daylight. The sun is up around 5:00 a.m. and sets a bit after 8:00 p.m. It's cool, but the parks are alight with daffodils. Planters bursting with red and pink geraniums hang from shop windows and decorate the pedestrian walkways throughout Oxford. Bright green lawns roll along the side streets and pathways to school. Such a canopy of life and light brings quiet tears of joy and regret. I feel so alive in this weather; we never have daffodils like these in Boston, much less even a spring; often we jump from winter to summer in New England.

But I'm still a bit sad. I would love to stay here, not just for another year, but perhaps forever. I've found parts of myself here that have been hidden away my whole life. The part of me that can be less of a perfectionist. The part of me that knows how to create a life for myself. The part of me that laughs at my mistakes and trusts God to carry me whether things are rough or breezy. This business of coming to terms with ourselves is not a walk in the park, but we need not be alone in it. By sharing with a trusted colleague or friend things we're ashamed of, things that confuse us, things we desperately desire, we learn to trust our intuition about how to become the person we are each called to be.

Enough musing. I must "get on"! There are eight weeks left to the school year and lots to do with the children. They are full of energy too. "Hallo, Ma! Did you have a nice holiday? Did you go back to America for a visit?" some of them ask as they bounce into class the first morning back to school.

"I had a lovely holiday. My husband and I spent time in Oxford and traveled to Salisbury and Dorset. I didn't go back to America."

In class, I point the children to five story starters on the whiteboard:

> *The room was dusty and dank . . .*
> *Watch out for . . .*
> *I can hardly wait for . . .*
> *I remember . . .*
> *When I visit my gran . . .*

"Pick one of these and write for fifteen minutes. Then each of you will read a paragraph or a few sentences aloud, so make sure you have something you feel comfortable sharing!" The children giggle and point to Jonathan, probably recalling when we did this exercise before, and he shared a silly scene about walking in on his aunt in the loo.

When I first arrived here, I struggled against my automatic impulse to walk around the classroom, looking at students' work, as I would have done at Fessenden. Such hands-on support helped the boys focus on their studies, but Dragon students don't need that, and they know that I have my own work to do. My dragons write, and I spent these fifteen minutes making notes on future plans for M3B. The room settles into love. Love for one's work. Love for the silent presence of others.

After the allotted time, I consider ringing my little bell, but the students are still deeply involved in their work. I take the pulse of the room.

Ding-a-ling, ding-a-ling, goes my bell. "M3B, you are quite engaged with your writing. Would you like to continue for another ten or fifteen minutes, or are you quite content to stop and share?"

Several kids call out, "Let's share!" So we do. Most of the kids have picked the writing prompts "Watch out for . . ." and "I remember. . . ." For the next half hour, we are treated to tales of hidden snakes, a trip to South Africa during term break, flying saucers, last season's rugby win over St. Edward's School, and sundry other moments in the lives of eleven-year-old girls and boys.

By the time all the children have shared, we have only a few minutes left. Naomi asks, "Ma, what were you doing while we wrote our stories? You looked like you were working on something important. Come on! Share with us."

At Fessenden, I would probably express my feelings about the "love" I felt in the classroom while they were all writing, but to share that here would break the strict boundary between student and teacher. Instead, I tell them, "I've been working on a special reading-and-writing project for you to do with the children from Lymans."

"Lymans!" The room rings out.

Then Davis shouts, "A lot of us came from Lymans. Hands up if you're a Lymans!"

Most of the class wave their hands. Some shout out, "Ma, tell us, tell us. What are we doing with Lymans kids?"

"Okay, everyone. Let's keep a lid on it." I wait for them to settle. "My idea is to start a reading-and-writing activity here at the Dragon with you as teachers of the Lymans children who will be students here next year. Lymans kids will come to our campus once a week during summer term to see what the Dragon is like before they arrive in the autumn. During these visits, each of you will read a book to several children and to help them write something about it. It's a chance for them to become familiar with our campus and classes and for you to be leaders."

Some of the kids say, "That's brilliant, Ma! Where did you get this idea?"

"I worked on a program like this with the sixth-grade boys at my school in Boston. Once a week, they read to the children in kindergarten, which here is called reception. This week we'll go to our library, and you can each check out three or four books you'd like to read to them. We'll start the visits next week."

The room fills with chatter about all the books these eleven-year-olds read when they came to the Dragon as nine-year-olds: *The Witches*, *The Little Prince*, *The Wolves of Willoughby Chase*, and *The Borrowers*.

Listening to these kids makes me realize how much I will miss their joie de vivre, how much I'll miss my colleagues and this school community—indeed, how much I'll miss England when I'm back in America—but right now I'm happy to be in this moment with these bubbly children talking about books. What more could an English teacher ask for?

Later that day, I head into Gunga Din to check my mailbox. As I round the corner out of the small, dingy mailroom, I see Betsy standing at the copy machine over in the far corner of the common room, her magnificent red hair twirled into a '50s-style bun on top of her head. She's got her back to me, and the machine is grinding out copies with its usual grunt. I'm not sure she's seen me come in. If she has, will she wait for me to tell her my decision about the two English positions or bring it up herself? I could skip out without her seeing me, but that would only put off the obvious. Besides, acclimated as

I may be to English ways, there are still a few of which I'm never certain, such as sussing out whether an English person will initiate a conversation or wait to be spoken to.

I cough loudly enough to be heard over the copy machine. Betsy whirls around on one of her black pumps. "Oh! Hallo, Barbara! Did you have a good holiday? And did you get my letter about applying for the positions here?"

Yup, right to the point. The Brits don't mess around with small talk about how your day is going.

"I had a wonderful holiday. Brady and I spent some time in Salisbury and Dorset. We saw Stonehenge. What a magnificent monument to the past," I say, hoping we can delay the inevitable.

Betsy steps away from the copy machine, looks pointedly at me, and says politely, "I'm glad you got to Stonehenge. It's one of our national treasures. Now, tell me about next year. Have you been able to think about whether you'll apply for one or both of the positions here?"

Ooh, her words sound like maybe I don't have to tell her my decision yet. I could tell her that I'm still thinking about it, since she's framed her question in that vein. But that feels wrong. And Brady has reminded me who I am. I have to take the risk of telling Betsy the truth, no matter how hard it may be. I don't like to disappoint people who think highly of me, but to tell Betsy anything else would be dishonest, and I could lose her good opinion of me. One thing I've learned here is not to promise what I can't deliver. It's not English, and, though I'm American, I hope I can take some of that particular Englishness back home with me.

I clear my throat and venture in, "Bets, I did receive your letter. Thank you for telling me about the positions. It's quite an honor to be asked to stay at the Dragon—"

Betsy's eyes light up. "Oh, jolly good! Does that mean you'll let me put your name forward to the search committee? I do hope so. We need you, Barbara. You are such a good colleague."

Oh, brother! This is not how I thought the conversation would go. I don't want to let her down. My comments just now were so American. I need to be more English and get to the point. Dear God, give me strength and give me the words.

Stepping toward her, I want to tell Betsy why I can't apply for the positions, but this is what comes out of my mouth: "Well, Bets, I have spent a good deal of time thinking about it. There are lots of wonderful reasons to stay—"

Betsy does a little hop in her heels. "Excellent! I'll tell the committee when we meet tomorrow."

I look around the small, windowless copy room and take a deep breath. A sudden calm prevails, and God gives me the words. "Bets! I can't stay. I would dearly love to, but I can't. Brady and I talked about this at length, and there are just too many unknown factors, which I won't bore you with, but essentially, I have a commitment to return to Fessenden and Brady has to return to his college. Nonetheless, it means the world to me that you and the committee think so much of me. Please thank them. If circumstances were different, I would apply for the positions." I look away, hoping she doesn't detect the small tears in my eyes. I thought I had put this behind me.

Betsy looks away too. For a second the room is silent. Then, in her quiet voice, she says, "I do understand. I thought this might be the case. I wanted to explore the possibility, as I didn't know for certain of your arrangement with Fessenden or Brady's agreement with his school. We will all be sorry to see you go. I hope you know that when you leave, you will forever be an old Dragon! All who come to the Dragon are ODs when they leave. You're part of the Dragon family and will always be welcome here. Who knows—maybe it will work out for you to come back and teach here another time!" Betsy throws her hands in the air when she offers this last sentence.

By now I'm really tearing up, but I swallow hard and smile. "Everyone has been so kind and helpful. I do feel as if the Dragon has become my home in so many ways. I will certainly come back to visit."

Betsy gathers up her papers, and as we leave the copy room together, she says, "Brilliant! Now, is there any chance you would consider taking the under-eleven girls' tennis team with me this term? It'll be fun to work together, and you know most of the girls."

I stop in the hallway. I'm not keen on coming home late after game practices and matches, as I observed other games takers do earlier in the year. I was glad not to have that additional responsibility at that point in my exchange. But I'm so settled here, and Betsy has asked most graciously. I want to give back to this wonderful community, as they have given to me. Besides, there's no pressure in her question, as there would have been at Fessenden ("We need an extra tennis coach this spring, and we want you to do it"). So it feels natural and good to say yes.

"Sure! I'd be happy to help. I'll be coaching the intramural tennis team at Fessenden when I return, so this will help me get back in tennis shape."

"Tremendous! I'll tell the head games taker." Then, glancing at her watch, straightening her bun, and adjusting her papers, she says, "Golly, look at the time. I have a class! Ta!" Betsy never does fewer than three things at once.

Walking home that afternoon, I have another aha moment: The book activity with M3B and being a tennis taker are similar to duties I enjoy at Fessenden. Maybe it won't be quite so hard to go back. I've missed coaching tennis with my colleague Cindy. She was so understanding and helpful after I broke my ankle two years ago. I had to sit during tennis practice, but she helped the boys to work with each other. I also want to beef up my reading program with the sixth-grade and kindergarten boys. Besides reading, they could do some service projects together.

The cool days of early May turn warmer, and the weather "breeds lilacs out of the dead land," as T. S. Eliot tells us in his epic poem *The Waste Land*. Students and staff abandon their winter gear and don cotton and linen clothes. The days are much longer. How delicious to have sunlit skies at 9:00 p.m.!

The weather inspires M3B. A group of them say, "Ma Kennard, it is very fine out; why not let us read to our Lymans students in the library garden when they come this afternoon?"

"With pleasure! Let's plan to meet here in the classroom first. Some of you can review our rules for having class outside, and then we can all walk to the garden." Given the Lymans kids' rambunctiousness and M3B's tendency to join in, I hope the latter will model their own words for the former.

Later that afternoon, Lucy announces to twenty-five nine-year-olds, "Now, boys and girls from Lymans, we can be outside today only if you mind your manners. No niggling your neighbor. No shouting or running about. Stay with your Dragon teacher. Right! Teachers and students, find each other and get reading!" Surprisingly, no one niggles, and all around the garden sit little and big children bent over books. Perhaps Lucy is a future teacher herself.

On the home front, Brady greets me one evening with a glass of chardonnay and announces, "I have some news. Nothing dramatic, but something we need to start attending to."

"That sounds cautious. What is it?"

Brady hands me a stack of papers. "These came in the mail today."

"Should I look at them while I'm eating?"

"I'll summarize them for you. These are papers from Finders Keepers, our letting agents, outlining what we have to do before leaving on July thirty-first. There's a handy checklist and some forms to fill out."

We look over the list of tasks to do, and Brady points out, "We'll need to pay June and July rent in June. I'll go down to Finders Keepers and pay the rent. Can you start packing up our winter clothes?"

"All right, but we'll also have to return Laura and Hans's television before they leave for Germany in mid-July. And what about all the kitchen things and decorations for the flat we bought but can't take back to the States? There's so much to think about and do all of a sudden."

"Barb, we don't have to do these things all at once, and I'll be able to do some while you're still teaching. Just so all this doesn't catch us on the back foot, let's make a calendar of what to do and when to do it. These next months will go by quickly. Before we know it, we'll be headed to Gatwick for our flight home."

I take a gulp of chardonnay and wipe my eyes on my sleeve. Brady looks at me and asks, "What's wrong?"

"I thought I'd accepted that we're going back to Boston, but I guess there's still some part of me that doesn't want to go. It's not just getting this list of stuff to do; it's hard to go because I'm having such a wonderful time at school. The kids and I are really in sync, and colleagues tell me how sorry they are that I have to leave. The idea of going back to Fessenden and Boston doesn't feel like going home, because the Dragon and Oxford feel like home to me now." I slump into the sofa.

Brady sits down next to me. "I understand. When I studied in

London at the Royal College of Music in 1969 and '70, I made lots of friends and had a hard time going back to the States. It took me a while to feel at home again, but the opportunity to do my doctorate at Boston University helped me settle in. You'll have opportunities at Fessenden that will help you settle in too."

"I arranged for this exchange because I wanted a different teaching experience, and I got it! I'm a different teacher from the teacher I was a year ago, but I'm going back to the same school I left. I don't see what opportunities I'll have there, and I don't know how or if I'll settle in. I don't want to go back to Boston or to Fessenden," I protest, throwing a sofa pillow across the room.

"Well, I do!" Brady says. Then he stands up and walks over to pick up the pillow.

"What's *that* supposed to mean?" I stand up.

Brady flings his hands in the air. "Look, Barbara, I love Oxford. I've had some once-in-a-lifetime experiences here too. Going to Romania was never going to happen in Quincy, Massachusetts, but you know we can't stay here. We've been through all this, and, despite the wonderful times I've had here, I don't want to stay in Oxford. I want to go home to Boston, where we have an equally wonderful, though different, life."

I walk to the big picture window and stand in front of it. *How often I have stood here without Brady to look out this window, the only window in the lounge? How often have I solved a problem or rejoiced in some accomplishment while standing here, gazing at the trees and the garden, rain or shine?*

Brady joins me. Turning to him, I admit, "I don't often see the forest for the trees, but you do. I guess I've been too busy thinking about how sublime it would be to stay here, when I already have such a wonderful life with you, no matter where we live."

We return to the sofa and sit. "Nothing is ever ideal, but we've had a very good life in Boston, and we will again when we return."

My other half is probably right, but getting past all the goodbyes is what will be so hard for me. And yet I remember waving goodbye to him from the departure lounge in Logan Airport on the last day of August 1998, knowing I wouldn't see him for four months and also knowing how much I wanted this exchange.

Brady gently squeezes my hand. "You're lost in your thoughts again, Barb,"

"Sorry. I hope after all I have experienced here that it will be a little easier for me to say goodbye to this place, but right now, going back to Boston and to Fessenden doesn't feel so great."

"Barb, you were fine about our departure until we started talking about all the things we have to do to leave."

My husband knows me well. "Okay. I'll let you tell me what we need to do when we need to do it. That might help me focus on school," I say, as I pick up the papers from the coffee table.

"That's the ticket, lovey. Enjoy these last weeks with the children and your colleagues," Brady says, and gives me a kiss. Then he takes the papers from the letting office and says, with a wry grin, "Better if I keep these and let you get on with your schoolwork."

I grin from ear to ear when he says, "that's the ticket," and he reads my mind: "We'll both be using English expressions for a long time to come. It'll help us remember all the good times we've had here. But don't get any ideas. We *are* going home!"

"I know. This isn't just about me—it's about us."

Brady and I hug each long and tight. Then he breaks away gently and goes to the guest room to put away the papers. Coming back into the lounge, he suggests we watch *One Foot in the Grave*, one of our favorite British sitcoms, about residents dealing with various ailments in a senior-living facility.

"Good idea. I'll make us some bowls of ice cream." A few minutes later, from the kitchen, I call out, "Gosh, you know, we'll miss *One Foot in the Grave* when we're back in Boston!"

No response from the lounge.

"And we'll surely *miss* all those other sitcoms we like: *Good Neighbors* and *Are You Being Served*?"

Still no reply. I take in the bowls of ice cream and put them on the coffee table.

Brady's standing up with a rather knowing look. In his best English accent, he says, "Sorry, love, that's very funny, but we're not staying here, not even for *One Foot in the Grave!*"

For a moment, neither of us says a thing. Then we both collapse on the sofa in laughter.

The first weeks of June pass uneventfully as we begin to complete our to-do lists. Brady pays our last two months of rent. I pack up our winter clothing, and we borrow a colleague's car to take the boxes to the post office. We also complete the most bothersome task on our list, taking the ten-mile round-trip bus ride to the BT office in Kidlington to fill out all the paperwork required to give up our phone. Doing this now will enable us to avoid the queues when we return with the phone at the end of July. How cumbersome! I won't miss this inconvenience when I'm back in the States. It's a good reminder of how much easier life can be there. Maybe there will be other things I will be happy to return to. Like driving to a supermarket. Our own television. A phone with an answering machine and caller ID. Our house and garden and Stanley. No doubt there will be other things about England that I won't miss.

—

It's here. July 16. My last day at the Dragon. It is the last morning assembly I will attend. The last time I will sing the school song, "Jerusalem." The last day I will see my colleagues and students. I'm walking aimlessly around our flat, looking for my school materials, when Brady gently hands me my lesson plan book and some of the kids' journals. I exhale and sink into the leather sofa. He sits and gives me a tissue. I dab my eyes, and for a moment we sit together quietly. Then I stand up and open the curtains of our big picture window to a canvas of green grass and pink roses. The sun blazes in. Brady helps me put on my rucksack and says, "I hope you have a really good last day of school."

"Thanks for your help, lovey." I kiss him. "Now, I must get on. I'll see you this afternoon at the Mitre for lunch."

Walking to school, I pass the usual collection of buses and cars filled with students, some from the Dragon, at a standstill in the bumper-to-bumper traffic all the way from the Summertown shops to the Oxford city center. I chuckle to myself as I realize that, once again, I'll probably arrive at school before the kids do.

At the school gate, children clamber out of cars, shouting and running into the schoolyard to play their last games of marbles or kickball. Teachers run about with all manner of stuff in their arms, calling to one another over the din of the children. How much this looks like that day I arrived in September. Actually, it's not much different from most first or last days at schools in the States.

Before going into Lymans Hall, I stop by Gunga Din and put thank-you notes in Debbie's, Betsy's, and Jenny's mailboxes. I thought to give them each a gift, but when I asked Robin Young his advice, he suggested, in the gentlest of words, "'Barbara, your gratitude has already been communicated in your good deeds and your hard work here. A brief thank-you note is best."

The assembly begins as Robin approaches the podium on the stage. He waits for the din of shouting students to die down before he speaks. "Welcome to the closing assembly of the 1998–'99 school year. Before we say goodbye to the 'leavers' class, I have a few remarks about the year in general. You know that these are always meant in good fun and that I cannot possibly speak about each child. The children I mention have been chosen at random, and their actions could easily apply to any of you.

"Henry W. won the school geography prize, so hopefully he will be able to find his form room next year."

Robust laughter from the audience.

These and other accolades offered are so endearingly English. The art of irony and gentle sarcasm is alive and well in this country.

Robin continues, "I could go on and on, but I won't. Suffice it to say that it was a very good year for many dragons and could have been better for some if they had tried a little harder. But there's always next year."

Another teacher comes forward to announce the last part of the assembly: skits that the children have prepared to memorialize various events of the school year. Some are funny, some express gratitude for certain moments in school life, and some are a bit off-color, but no one seems to mind. Just when they seem to be over, ten boys and girls parade out from backstage and stand in a semicircle with their right hands behind their backs. They are wearing red, white, and blue shirts. Maybe they're going to sing some English songs? Someone blows a whistle, and they all bring their right hands out from behind them. And now I know I'm in trouble. Each kid holds a small American flag.

George, one of my rowdier dragons from Upper 2B, steps forward and calls out, "Ma Kennard, come on down!"

Some of the kids hoot, "Ma Kennard! Ma Kennard!"

Then Denise, Thomas, and Derek from my Lower 2A class—the same class I told to get their willies out—take my hand and walk me to the stage. I try to smile, but, based on what the headmaster just said about some of the students, I'm a little uncertain what these kids are up to. Once onstage, I am escorted to a chair decorated like a throne and asked to sit down. Andy, one of my Upper 5 boys, gently places a gold paper crown on my head.

Then it happens. To the tune of the American musical *Bye Bye Birdie*, the kids onstage sing this song:

Oh, Ma Kennard,

sometimes you drove us crazy,

　Do they know how much they drove me *crazy?*

but if you're not near us, we'll be lazy.

Oh, Ma Kennard,

we'll miss you.

Oh, Ma Kennard,

sometimes you didn't have a clue.

　Was it that obvious?

But if you're not near us, we'll be blue.

Oh, Ma Kennard,

we'll miss you.

Oh, Ma Kennard,

exam prep was rough,

but when you're not near us, life'll be tough.

Oh, Ma Kennard,

we'll miss you!

　And I'll miss all of you too.

Whistling and clapping follow. More of my students from Upper 5 and M3B hop up onstage and read notes they've written on the yellow "praise slips" teachers give to deserving students for accomplishments.

"Thanks, Ma Kennard, for being a great form taker. We had lots of laughs with you after you got used to us," Madeline says.

Sally jumps in: "Ma Kennard, I will miss the orange that you brought to school and put on your desk every morning." She hands me an orange.

"Thank you, Ma Kennard, for helping me when my mum was sick. I will miss you," Harriet says softly.

Then Annie and Sara step up. "It was fun having you take us for tennis and when you went with our history class to Warwick Castle."

Finally, the entire group shouts out, "Ma Kennard, you're a really cool teacher—for an American."

Thankfully, the skits and speeches are over, but the children clearly delighted in this chance to "take the mickey" out of me, so this is *my* chance to be the different teacher I've become here and not take these remarks personally. *Remember the plastic turd!* I tell myself. *Barbara, if you could handle that, you can handle this public display of genuine affection for you and who the children see you as.*

Robin looks at me with a gleam in his eyes and says, "Ma Kennard, we salute you, a fine American teacher who has taught English to English children very well. We will miss you. We wish you good luck on your return to Fessenden. And remember that you are an old dragon, and old dragons are vital to our life here. Do come back and visit."

Everyone in the hall claps for me. It's not raucous applause; no one hoots or hollers. Despite the kids' ribbing, since the headmaster has complimented me in a formal and serious fashion, the rest of the auditorium responds in like manner. So, not in spite of my students' teasing but because of it, I smile and wipe away a tear at their commendations. After spending the year working with all these kids and colleagues, they trust that I will not take their sardonic comments personally. I am one of them now. Funny how much this kind of humor used to bother me when I first arrived here. Perhaps I've learned not to take myself so seriously.

After all the cleanup is finished, library books returned, "bits and bobs" collected from the lost-property box, and uniforms chucked in the games bins, my form returns to the classroom to say their formal goodbyes—something the school still holds on to, even in the last year of the twentieth century.

In another delightful example of the unconventional at the Dragon, my form lines up in alphabetic order by their first names. There's the usual scuffle between Christopher and Christopher as to who will be first. I stand by the open door, knowing I probably won't see these kids again, so I want their last image of me to be a happy one. I say a quick, quiet prayer to myself and extend my right hand. Each child steps forward and gives me a firm handshake. Each one says, "Goodbye, Ma Kennard. Thank you for being my form taker." As each child looks me directly in the eye and speaks these words, I recognize the many different inflections in each voice that make this otherwise ubiquitous statement so personal, as if no one else has ever said goodbye and thank you to me before this moment. How often do we hear the same words over and over and conclude that such repetition feels meaningless? We resent it when someone's words aren't exclusive to us. Instead, we should listen for the uniqueness of each voice and hear love in that sound. Besides, repetition is a good thing; we need to hear or do something at least seven times before we can begin to understand it.

I walk with my form to the school gate, which is jammed with parents and grandparents waiting to collect their charges. All the children walk through the gate, some for the last time. I turn to head back to my room to collect my belongings, when Jenny, Betsy, and Debbie come up and ask, "Do you have plans for lunch, Barbara?"

"Gosh, I do, as it were. Brady and I are having lunch at the Mitre in town and then we're catching the fourteen-thirty train to London for the weekend."

My three friends usher me away from the gate to a quieter place under the big maple tree by the administration building. They gather around me in small circle, and Jenny pulls a book from her bag. "We thought you might like a copy of this year's *The Dragon Book of Verse*," she says, as she hands me a small yellow-and-blue book with a picture of a friendly dragon on the cover.

Debbie looks at me with a twinkle in her blue eyes and tells me, "I think you'll especially enjoy some of the poems your Upper 5 class wrote."

"And look on page twenty-four for the song the children sang to you today." Betsy laughs, throwing back her head. Whenever she does that, I wonder if her bun will come undone, but it never does.

For a minute, I look away and swallow hard. Then I softly clear my throat and offer, "My goodness, this is so kind of you. Thank you so much. I'm sorry I can't do lunch today. But we're here until the end of July. Perhaps we could all meet up for lunch sometime next week?"

Jenny looks at Betsy and Debbie and says, "That would be lovely, but I think we're all off on our holidays next week. Most of us try to avoid traveling in August because of the heat, not to mention all the tourists from—"

"America?" I joke, and all four of us laugh.

"Well, yes. Present company excluded!" Debbie says.

"No worries. I tend to avoid American tourists myself. Well, then

I guess this is goodbye," I say, as I put the poetry book in my bag. There's a moment of silence between us, and part of me worries that I've ended our encounter too quickly. Maybe I should have said more about how much they mean to me and how grateful I am for their friendship, but I've done that in my notes, and it's time to go, for me and for them. I step toward these three wonderful women with my arms outstretched. They already have theirs in the air, and for a second we might be mistaken for Dragon kids in the schoolyard. We give each other a good squeeze, say goodbye and good luck, and wave as we part company.

That's it. No dragged-out, gooey farewells. How refreshing it can be to speak and hear straightforward words when we take our leave. Even significant ones need not be maudlin to be sincere. Betsy crosses Charlbury Road and walks toward Summertown. Jenny heads to the car park. Debbie walks to the library to return her books. Each of us must get on to the next thing. I look at my watch. It's already half twelve. Brady will be wondering where I am; we were meant to meet at noon. Turning away from the Dragon, I hurry to catch the number 7 bus for the city center.

At the Mitre, Brady waves to me. I hurry over. "Lovey, I am so sorry I'm late; one thing led to another this morning at school, and then I got caught up with Betsy, Debbie, and Jenny at the end."

Brady puts down his book. "That's okay. I thought this might happen, so I ordered for us. Our lunches should be here soon. So, how was your last day at the Dragon?"

"It was lovely. The kids wrote and performed a sweet skit about me, and Betsy, Jenny, and Debbie gave me a copy of this year's edition of *The Dragon Book of Verse*."

I pull it out of my bag and hand it to him. He leafs through it, and I point out the song they wrote about me.

We eat and discuss what we want to do on our last trip to London. After a little while, Brady asks, without looking up at me, "So, was it hard to leave today?"

I swallow my mouthful of toad in the hole and say, "I tossed and turned last night, wondering what this day would be like. This morning I was in a bit of a muddle and couldn't get myself together. But once I got to school and jumped into all the chaos, I didn't have time to get sad about this being my last day."

"So, does that mean you're ready for the next big thing?" Brady asks, with a twinkle in his eye but a serious tone in his voice. He drinks his water and pouts, as if to say, *I know this is a hard question.*

I push my food around the plate and acknowledge, "If you mean am I ready to go back to the States and to teaching at Fessenden, I hope so. That's not to say I'm super excited to go back, but I think I'll be ready when the time comes. It helped that everyone around me today was ready to leave. People here don't drag out farewells; they're all about getting on with the next thing, and I mean to do that too."

Brady smiles and leans over to kiss me. "I'm so glad. Now, let's eat up and hustle over to the station to catch our train to London."

After our last weekend in London, we return to Oxford to attend to the last of our "leaving" chores. The day before we depart, I make one last visit to the Dragon School.

Ambling down Hernes Road to Lonsdale Place, I see the familiar leafy path that takes me past St Edmund's cricket grounds to Marston Ferry Road. At MFR, I walk under the overpass and cross to St Frideswide School. From there, I travel the path bordering the empty tennis courts to the new development of posh single-family homes on Charlbury Road. On the corner of Charlbury and Belbroughton

Roads sits the venerable Oxford School for Girls. The Dragon is close by now. I turn left onto Belbroughton Road and walk to the corner of Bardwell Road, where Gunga Din greets me. I push open the old wooden gate and step onto campus. No one is here. Not even a dorm parent or someone in the administration building. Golly, Debbie was right about everyone taking off for their holidays!

I take out my camera and snap a picture of Gunga Din, where teachers had coffee at ten and drinks "not a minute before five." Across from Gunga looms the high tower with the iron bell rung each morning for bun break by a young dragon. If I were bold, I would ring it now, but that is never an adult's job. I step far enough away to photograph the whole tower. Then I turn to the west. Majestic and alone, the school's monument to all the ODs who died in the Great War stands in empty green fields. I hear all seven hundred members of the Dragon community singing "Jerusalem" during our Remembrance Day service last November 11,1998. And it is in this moment that I know, like all the thirteen-year-olds at the Dragon, I too am a "leaver." It is time to go back to Boston and to Fessenden. I've accepted that I have to go, but that doesn't diminish how much I'll miss this place. Yet over this sadness, hope rises. Hope that my Fessenden colleagues will be happy to see me; hope that I'll be able to set more doable expectations for myself and my students; hope that eventually I'll recover from missing the Dragon and my life here. Nonetheless, just beneath these hopes lives a worry about something that's troubled me for much of my teaching career: fitting in at American schools. Will I be able to reacclimate to Fessenden? As I walk away from the war monument, W. H. Auden's poem "In Memory of Sigmund Freud" comes to mind. Auden suggests that with all our weaknesses, we can only hope "to improve a little by living." I don't think Auden would mind if I amended that line to "improve a little by teaching."

—

Brady and I stand blurry-eyed at gate 29A in Gatwick Airport at 5:30 a.m. on July 31, waiting for our 7:30 a.m. flight to Boston. When a Virgin Atlantic flight attendant announces that our flight has been delayed by an hour, I spot a Pret-à-Manger nearby and walk over to get us some food. As I stand in line to pay, I overhear some American students talking about their return to the United States. They look young, maybe late teens or early twenties. Their chatter takes me back to my own memories of coming to this country eleven months ago.

I was so excited and so nervous on that last day of August 1998 as I boarded a Virgin Atlantic flight to cross the pond and teach at the Dragon School. "Anxious" also describes my feelings as I deplaned in this same airport. Alone, with two heavy suitcases and only a vague idea of what lay ahead, I hoped for a once-in-a-lifetime experience that would reinvigorate me in radical ways. I had lots of expectations and goals, as we teachers know how to create. I've realized some of them, though not solely on my own merit and rather through the grace of God and my decision to say yes to these changes. Yet I know even my yes hasn't come without the nudging and prodding of the Holy Spirit.

Looking across from Pret-à-Manger, I see people in our gate area gathering their belongings. The flight attendant has her microphone in hand. "Ladies and gentlemen, we will be boarding VA flight 4476 to Boston in about twenty minutes. Please have your tickets ready. Thank you for your patience, and thank you for flying Virgin Atlantic."

I look over to see Brady waving madly at me, wearing a big grin. He's so happy to be going back home. Back home. I've not used that phrase much in the last few months, but it sounds good, and it feels right.

Chapter 9
Back in the USA

After we make our way through customs and immigration at Logan Airport, we hail a taxi, only to be told that we have too much luggage for one cab. Brady suggests that I take a cab with our carry-on luggage; he'll follow in another one with the bigger cases.

My cab driver takes me the usual route through downtown Boston onto the Southeast Expressway. As we drive over the Neponset Bridge and onto Quincy Shore Drive, some familiar haunts come into view: Marina Bay, where we had dinner on the dock; Dunkin' Donuts; and a local ice cream shop. I remember them, yet now I feel as if I'm seeing them for the first time. After we pass CVS, the road takes the turn I always looked for each day I drove home from Fessenden, because at this point in the journey, I knew I was almost there. Now the road straightens and runs parallel to Quincy Bay. Beyond the bay lies the great Atlantic I just flew over. We are less than ten minutes from our house. My palms sweat. *Maybe the driver will catch some of the red lights on this road.* But no, he sails through all of them. Before I know it, he turns to me and says, "Here we are, eight Victoria Road! Welcome home." He leaps out of the cab, gets the cases from the trunk, and looks at me curiously. I roll down the window as he asks, "Is this the right house?"

"Uh-huh," I reply.

My driver places the carry-on luggage on the front porch and comes back to open the taxi door for me. I look toward our house and then at the bay across the street. Then I undo my seat belt and look around for my rucksack.

The driver looks at his watch and says, "Miss, I have another ride to pick up."

I'm looking in my rucksack for my house key when he asks, "Do you need help getting out of the cab?"

"No, but just let me find my keys," I say.

My driver begins pacing around the car. He looks at me and taps his wristwatch.

I can't find my keys, but I'll have to let him get on with his next ride. I place both my feet on the driveway, and the driver extends his hand to help me out. We walk up the front steps. I turn to him and quietly say, "Thank you. I can manage now." He runs down the steps, leaps into his cab, and roars off.

I gaze around the neighborhood. All the lawns are green, their gardens in full bloom, just like the properties on Hernes Road in Summertown. But the houses are bigger here, and there are no flat buildings like our Oxford one. I lean against the porch railing for a minute. *Our flat building. A year ago, I stood in front of Westgate Grove on Hernes Road with another cab driver, who also helped me with my luggage.*

A truck clatters down Victoria Road, and I realize I must look a bit daft standing in front of my house, sussing out the neighborhood as if I were just moving in.

I shake myself and rummage through the cases for my house keys. I check my rucksack again and find them in a pocket, along with some old number 7 ticket stubs from the Oxford Coach Bus Company. I look out at Quincy Bay, wondering when Brady will get here. *Maybe I should wait for him to come. No, I have to get on with that "next big thing," unlock this door, and go into our house here in Quincy, Massachusetts.*

I struggle to get the keys into the lock and wipe my hands on my skirt. I try again and again and finally unlock the door. Inside the vestibule, I put down one of my cases and open the door to the living room. Stepping in, I hear Stanley meowing at the top of the stairs. He looks down at me as if to say, *'Bout time you came home. Where have you been?*

"Stanley!" I call out. He leaps down the stairs and winds himself around my ankles, like he did when I left here a year ago. I pick him up and listen to his big, loud purr. We walk around the house a bit, until he jumps out of my arms and runs to Brady, who has just walked through the front door. He comes over to where I'm standing in our dining room, takes me in his arms, and asks, "How does it feel to be home?"

I hug him and whisper, "It's okay. I'm glad to see Stanley and the bay, but being here takes me back to when I first arrived at our home in Oxford almost a year ago. It's bittersweet, but I'll be all right."

It's August 14, 1999. Brady and I have been back from our year abroad for two weeks. Sitting in our sunlit den, I rest in a leather recliner and gaze at the waters of Quincy Bay. I'm glad those weeks are over. I cried through some of it as I adjusted to a much faster pace of life in Boston and remembered how to drive a car. Ironic that only a month ago, I looked forward to being able to drive myself to the grocery store. *No more walking the one-mile round trip to the grocery stores in Summertown every other day*, I thought. But that was then. Now I walk to the Stop and Shop, a mile from our house, to slow down my day and revisit the experience of walking for more than exercise. I love strolling past the seventeenth-century Merrymount Cemetery and the colonial Congregational church on the way to the market. On these daily walks, it seems bizarre that Americans jog or walk to shed a few pounds, only to drive a mile to buy a quart of milk. Why not walk to the store and lose some of those extra pounds while enjoying the sights along the way?

August moves toward September, and I have less time to walk. Still, Brady and I cling to one of the most precious moments from our Oxford days: afternoon tea. We pledge to take time to slow down, talk about our day, and savor being together. Brady appears in our den with tea and sets the tray down on the wrought-iron table between our recliners. We sip in silence for a few minutes.

I turn to look again at the bay outside the wide picture windows and say, "You know, while I was in England, I didn't think about this bay or our lovely view of it, but now that I'm back, I realize how much I love sitting here, looking at the water."

He too has missed this aspect of our neighborhood, and we add other things we're glad to have back in our lives: Access to Boston via public transportation is quick and easy, and the South Shore Plaza isn't as quaint as the Oxford shops, but its variety of stores under one roof make shopping more efficient. Brady reaches across the table and takes my hand. "It's good to realize all that we have here."

I smile as he slips off to his piano to practice some Debussy. Feasting on the bay, I sit quietly and listen to him play. I don't need to distract myself with busy work. It's good to see my neighbors, to hear all the children playing their summer games, to get dirty in the garden again. And I do love August; its quintessential light, the harbinger of autumn, turns the bay into deep blue. My favorite season is not far off. And neither is the start of school. School. I didn't expect this feeling, but as I sit here with the bay and the August light, my thoughts turn to Fessenden and a new school year. I'm curious. *Is anyone around on campus? Maybe I should drive over there and find out? It'll be good to remember the way to school, even if no one is there.*

The next day, the route to Fessenden comes back easily. After the usual thirty-five-minute drive, I turn into the school's entrance and park in the empty faculty lot. The grounds are fresh, red and yellow mums massed along walkways. Workers on ladders repair some of the outdoor lighting fixtures; doors and school signs have been refreshed with new paint. I walk around to the middle-school entrance, but the doors are locked and the halls dark. Peering through the library's glass doors, I find no sign of life.

A workman passes by and asks, "Can we help you?"

"No, thanks. I was just curious to see if any faculty or administrators are around. I teach here."

"Just a few of us maintenance people working to get the place ready for the opening of school. No one else is around until the end of the week," he offers.

"Okay, good to know. By the way, the grounds look lovely," I mention.

"Appreciate you noticing!" he says. He waves and walks towards the Building and Grounds office, where a few trucks are parked.

I stroll through the leafy quad that cuts between Hathaway House, a dorm for ninth-grade boys, and the dining hall. Then I recognize it: the bench where I talked with John, the assistant headmaster, in the spring of 1997 and learned about the Dragon School exchange. I stop and look around at these same trees, the same benches, the same rose gardens under the dormitory windows, now filled with mums. I walk to that bench and sit. As I stare at the empty dorm and the empty visitors' parking lot nearby, a sudden feeling creeps over me, and I laugh right out loud. *How ironic that a little more than two years ago, in June 1997, I sat here and told John how I thought Fessenden wasn't a good fit for me. How unhappy I was teaching here. And now I'm here again, alone again. No one to greet me or to talk to.*

A maintenance truck zooms by, as if to remind me that it will not do to wallow in the past. I'm a different person and a different teacher now, and perhaps the folks at Fessenden are different too. Then a loud drilling sound screams from the nearby tennis courts. Some birds flit out of trees and float effortlessly to who knows where. I follow them as they take me down the hill to the middle-school building where I teach and toward my car in the faculty parking lot.

As I drive home, I tell myself, *So what if no one was there to greet me? So what if I didn't fit in at Fessenden in the past? That doesn't matter now. There is much to hope for: new friendships, new colleagues, and the chance to practice the new things I've learned at the Dragon School about myself and about good teaching.*

It's a great thing to be able to take the long view of our lives. We do well to be thankful for our struggles, countercultural though that is. When we give thanks for hard times, we create opportunities to learn more about who we are and how to reinvent ourselves. Above all, we should keep in mind St. Paul's hopeful admonition to always be looking forward, not backward.

What remains of August passes quickly as Brady and I jump back into life in Massachusetts. We work in our garden and take walks on the beach. Brady prepares to start college classes at the end of the month, and I work on lesson plans for the opening week of school after Labor Day.

On Tuesday, September 7, 1999, our first faculty meeting begins at nine o'clock, but I'm here at eight, familiarizing myself with Cahners Hall, the new home of Fessenden's middle school, built while I was on exchange. No one seems to be around; the hallways and middle-school office are still dark, except for a bulletin board with pictures of kids engaged in various activities around the school. I smile at the photos of them playing lacrosse on the upper fields, working in the new technology lab, singing in music class.

The classrooms are still locked, but I find mine, room 114, and peek through the narrow window in the door. My desk and the students' desks lie helter-skelter around the room. The bulletin boards are empty, and books sit any old way on the shelves, instead of resting in neat rows by genre. *I'll fix that*, I tell myself, and begin to imagine different ways to arrange my classroom this year.

Taking in the scope of this cluttered Fessenden classroom jolts me back to my rambunctious Upper 5 class at the Dragon. I hear their raucous scenes from *Slake's Limbo* and see my hat, used as a turban, lying in the corner under a window. The scattered chairs in *this* classroom look just like the subway scene Upper 5 created with their chairs. In our dingy yellow classroom a million miles away, a million years ago, I hear Sam say, *Hey, Ma, please, have you got any American coins we can use?*

Some Fessenden teachers' voices in a nearby hallway jolt me out of my reverie. It's eight forty-five, so I head to Cahners Auditorium for the nine o'clock meeting, hoping to catch up with some colleagues.

Inside the auditorium, Josh is working in the new tech booth, setting up slides. I call out to him with the usual September greeting teachers give to one another: "Hey, Josh, how was your summer? Are you ready for a new school year?" He gives me a smile and a quick wave. He must have a lot to do, so I go to the faculty room for some coffee and head back to the auditorium. On the way, I think about my

Dragon students and colleagues. I miss the kids' childlike innocence, which made them so lovable, despite, or maybe because of, their occasional bad behavior. I miss my Dragon colleagues popping into my classroom to say hello or to ask how things were going after I'd been out with a bad cold. I miss . . .

Stop! I tell myself. *Barbara, don't get caught up in these memories. You're back at Fessenden, and you must get on.* Still, I suddenly want to throw up and run to the nearest ladies' room. Once I'm safely inside a stall, the nausea dissipates, but then I burst into tears. When I sense someone else in the bathroom, I flush the toilet to disguise my crying. I wait. She uses the toilet, washes her hands, and rummages in a bag. Finally, she leaves. I exit my stall and hear voices from the hallway. Sounds like the meeting is finally getting under way. I splash cold water on my face, check that my eyes aren't too red, and head into Cahners.

Back in the auditorium, teachers chatter about their summers and their joy about the new school year. Fred Post ambles over to the speaker's podium at the front of the stage, and the crimson curtains part to reveal a huge screen being electronically lowered into place.

"Good morning, Fessy teachers! We'll start our opening meeting in a few minutes. Everyone, please find a seat," Fred calls.

Chitchat continues as seventy-five teachers look for places to sit. I see three colleagues nearby and wave to them to come over, but they turn away and sit with their science colleagues on the other side of the aisle.

I walk over to a nearby empty space in the auditorium to clear my head and quiet my heart. Then I take a seat in the first row of chairs near the podium and try to understand their reaction. Come to think of it, these three were part of a group of teachers who didn't join in the celebration of my exchange in June 1998. I had forgotten all that until now. I hope they'll be able to overcome whatever negative feelings they had then and be collegial.

My thoughts are interrupted by Saskia, one of the history teachers who's been at Fessenden for most of her career. She slides up next to me and remarks, "Oh, Barbara. So, you're back," as if I've just done something naughty.

Hmm, being back doesn't sound like a good thing, but I'll give Saskia the benefit of the doubt. Standing up, I smile and say, "It's so great to see you, Saskia. Have a seat."

Saskia glares at me. "I'm not sure this exchange was such a good idea for Fessenden. Maybe it was for you, but you're just one person. You know these things have to work for the whole school. You may have had a good experience, but I have to say that the guy who took your place wasn't much of a teacher."

"Gosh, I'm sorry you feel that way."

"Jim was often away from school. When some of us talked to Fred about his absences, Fred said the exchange experience included traveling around the United States. Jim also didn't do any of your book projects or the writing exercises the boys need. And no Shakespeare! I would have thought that a teacher from England would do something with Shakespeare, but when the boys asked if they'd be acting out scenes from some of the plays, like you do each year, Jim didn't know how to orchestrate it."

With that, Saskia flips her long blond ponytail into a defiant swing and saunters off. She takes a seat with Tom. *What an odd idea. Does Saskia actually think I had anything to do with Jim's mistakes or successes here? Just as I was responsible for my efforts at the Dragon, so was Jim for his here.*

She doesn't come out and say it, but I sense from Saskia's accusatory tone that she thinks the school gave me special treatment in allowing me to do the exchange with Jim. Did his absences affect my colleagues' workloads? That could have been hard on teachers, since we're all so overloaded anyway. Or perhaps some teachers felt as if Jim wasn't held to the same standards as the rest of the faculty. I can see how they might have been disappointed that he didn't have to do what I did at Fessenden.

Fred fiddles with the microphone and clears his throat. I look for a different place to sit so that I'm not near him, as this might reinforce the possibility that Saskia thinks he favors me. Do other colleagues share her feelings? I consider moving to the back of the auditorium, but two teachers I don't know join me. It would be rude to move now. I introduce myself. "Hi, I'm Barbara Kennard, and I teach sixth-grade English."

A tall young woman with a blond pixie haircut gives me a delicate handshake. "I'm Katy Moore. I'll be teaching seventh-grade science. I'm new this year."

The other teacher, a short, older woman, reaches across Katy and grasps my hand firmly. "Nice to meet you, Barbara. I'm Brenda Davidson, the new seventh- and eighth-grade English teacher." Her introduction reminds me that the teacher she's replacing took a position at a school in Connecticut the same year I went to England. He and I were part of each other's professional evaluations and comrades in arms teaching grammar and writing.

I glance up at the ceiling for a second and get a grip before I reply, "Great to meet you both. I'm sort of new, but not really. I was away last year on a teaching exchange."

Fred begins the meeting: "Welcome back, everyone. I hope you all had a relaxing summer and are ready to hit the ground running. The boys will be here Thursday, and we have lots to do. Before we get into today's meetings, I'd like to welcome back a few people who have been away. When I call your name, please stand."

Fred continues by acknowledging two teachers who took off part of the previous year to finish their master's degrees, and the auditorium breaks into robust applause and hooting. Now it's my turn. What will Fred say about me? Will I get a rousing round of applause? Here it comes. Fred is looking at me. He smiles as he says, "And we're glad to have Barbara Kennard back from her exchange at the Dragon School last year. Barbara, we're excited to hear about all your adventures in England."

As I stand, a moment of silence echoes in the auditorium, followed by some quiet, conciliatory applause. I smooth the back of my skirt and slowly lower myself into my seat. After my interaction with Saskia and the other teachers who ignored my invitation to sit with me, my emotions bubble up, but I say a quiet prayer to myself: *Dear God, help me to put into practice some of what I learned at the Dragon School, including not to take these kinds of things personally.*

I imagine what some of my colleagues might say to me: *So, Barbara, why did you get to have a teaching exchange after only five years here? Some of us have been at Fessenden for twice as long as you have, and we've never had such an opportunity.*

And I might reply, *I'm sorry you feel that way. My exchange really had more to do with what I needed to do to grow as a teacher and much less with how long I've been here.*

Though they haven't yet said anything to me, I'm hoping Sally and Ellie, two teachers who supported my exchange and with whom I've worked on committees, will continue to be supportive colleagues.

I am jolted out of my thoughts by chairs scraping the floor. The faculty meeting is over, and everyone leaves the auditorium for lunch. I don't know what to do. If I sit at a table with others, they might ignore me. I look around for Brenda and Katy but don't see them. I don't want to eat alone, so I head to my classroom to set up for the first day of school. Decorating my room will give me a purpose for this afternoon.

Tucked away in my room, I begin to cover three large bulletin boards in yellow paper with red and orange paper leaves scattered over the two end boards. It brings back memories of some of my own teachers' classrooms, so spacious and bright, neat and orderly. My first-grade teacher, Miss Gluding, always had all kinds of stuffed animals around her room. She invited her students to hold one as we looked at picture books or listened to her read aloud. I couldn't wait to get to school when I was in first grade.

On the center board of my own classroom, I cluster a few leaves around a favorite pun illustrated in big, sparkly letters:

WELCOME TO SIXTH-GRADE ENGLISH!
WE'RE F
       A
        L
         L
          I
           N
             G   INTO A NEW SCHOOL YEAR!

Artistic and inspirational posters hang on the other walls. Monet's *Autumn Haystacks* invokes the in-between time of late summer and early fall. The others, DIFFICULTIES ARE STEPPINGSTONES TO SUCCESS and AN ERROR IS NOT A MISTAKE UNLESS YOU REFUSE TO CORRECT IT, will inspire the boys and me to our best work over the next nine months.

Next, I decide to rearrange the furniture. When I've finished, my large metal desk looks across the room toward the door, instead of hiding in a corner in the back of the room. Three bookshelves are tucked under the windows, which warm the room with southern light. A small couch nestles between the closet and the door. In the center of the room, fifteen shiny desks in three rows of five face the whiteboard.

It feels good to be doing this work, to make my mark again at Fessenden. I have so many hopes for this year: teaching Shakespeare again, investigating technology, and sharing some of the curriculum I used at the Dragon. But will my decorated classroom and all these plans be enough to return me to the hearts of teachers and students here?

After the opening days of school in September, I feel welcomed back by a few colleagues. Sally and Ellie suggest we have coffee from time to time in the faculty room. One day, Ellie joins me for lunch and expresses her interest in doing the exchange herself. Mandy, this year's intern, inspires me to keep moving forward with his ideas for doing some team teaching with me. I will be his mentor this year, and he'll need me to be available and not preoccupied with my own stuff. But apart from occasional interactions with these colleagues, I spend much of September alone, though it isn't as hard as one might think. Fessenden asks me to write an article for the school magazine about my experience at the Dragon, and I take consolation in devoting time to my students and my teaching. I have my memories of the Dragon, but as time goes by they become less painful to recall.

October 1999. Fessenden has been back in session for almost a month; the boys have settled into the daily sixth-grade routine of homeroom, classes, study hall, and sports, so it feels like a good time to do something a little out of the ordinary. I push desks haphazardly around the room. Some face the windows; others, the whiteboard. A few end up across the back of the room or sit diagonally in the middle.

The boys bounce in. Their usual hallway energy simmers down when they see the results of my interior decorating. Billy is excited. "Wow, Mrs. Kennard, what's with the desks?"

"I've been thinking it would be fun to take a break from our regular work and do something I taught the Dragon students last year, so I've rearranged the room to give each of you some space to think and write."

"Does it matter where we sit?" Joe wonders.

"Not at all."

Some of the boys walk around the room, surveying the arrangement of desks. Others rush to the same desks and have a bit of a scuffle over who gets there first. Rather than wait for the whole class to settle, I employ a Dragon tactic and get started. I'm happy when this approach encourages those who are lollygagging to get with it.

"Boys, here's something I hope will be fun for you," I say, and turn to write the following on the board:

> Write a one-page description of a recent vacation you had, in the voice of a place, an object, or a person you encountered on your vacation. But don't identify the "voice." Let your readers try to figure that out!

Now the room is abuzz with excitement, though the boys are talking mostly to each other about the first part of the assignment and not much about the "voice" part.

"Any questions?"

No one raises his hand.

"Okay. Let's get started." Then I remember to use an Americanism to motivate them: "I am excited to see what you will write."

The boys rummage around in their desks and binders to locate paper and pencils and begin.

At the Dragon, I learned to let my students wrestle with something new for a bit before checking on them, so I find some quiet tasks to do around the room while the boys try to write. However, within minutes, most of them form a line at my desk and wait for me to help them, although some of them have generated little or no writing.

I gently hold my ground. "Boys, I have confidence in you. You can do this assignment. The part about not revealing the 'voice' may be new to you, but it's important for each of you, and for me as your teacher, to see what you can do by yourselves. I'll come around in fifteen minutes to see how you're progressing."

The notion of "what you can do by yourselves" has become a challenge for many of us. It's such a human thing to be in partnership, especially when we're tackling something new or difficult. It's fun and can establish community when we learn together. And yet we should also ask what we are denying ourselves when we do the majority of our work or learning in groups. What would it feel like for each of us to accomplish a task independently, for how do we know what we are capable of on our own unless we are expected to produce that in some way?

The boys amble back to their desks. The next fifteen minutes crawl by. I would not have had to set up my expectations for the Dragon kids in this way. They would have found it odd, even annoying, to have me hanging around, waiting to look at their work. But that's probably because the Dragon students were used to writing every day in all their classes, not just English.

I feel my Fessy boys' expectations and get up from my desk to busy myself rearranging bookshelves and posters on the walls. Difficult as it is for the boys and for me, for I feel as if I'm dangerously close to those old accusations of demanding too much from them, I wait out the fifteen minutes. Then I begin to visit each boy. A few have attempted to camouflage the identity of their object, person, or place, but most have skipped that part of the assignment and have written only about their vacation. The assignment is probably too complex, given that I've not spelled it out, as I used to for almost every assignment. They need something more straightforward.

A few days later, for their Friday writing assignment, we try another Dragon assignment that I hope will be more accessible to my students. This time, I have the assignment already written on the whiteboard, in hopes that this will help them settle in sooner. My strategy works. When the boys come in, they see the assignment, find a desk, and take out their writing notebooks.

"Good morning, boys. Here's another assignment, which I hope you will find more doable than the one we attempted earlier this week. Let's try it. Michell, would you please read it out loud?"

Michell puts on his glasses and reads, "Choose one of the topics below and write a three hundred–word essay—that's about two pages—during this class period to express your opinion. Use examples from history or your personal experience to support your thinking and remember to include the opposing point of view as well. You will have all of class time to write."

The boys dig in with pretty good energy. I remind them, "I will collect your papers at the end of class to assess them. Spelling, punctuation, and grammar count! Do your best work!"

It's hard to pursue change, but we must adapt to be successful and to enjoy the fruits of our labor. In the end, it's not about getting everything right; what matters is that we keep trying and remain faithful to what we hope to accomplish.

My students eye these popular Dragon School topics with interest:

> *1. Everyone should play competitive sports.*
> *2. Television is good for you.*
> *3. Adults do not know best.*

I check in with them: "Does anyone have a question about what I'm asking you to do today?"

One boy calls out, "Are we gonna be able to finish these at home?"

Another asks, "What about spelling and grammar? Are you gonna correct that for us?"

"I would like to see what you can do in class, so you won't be able to finish the exercise at home this time. It's also important that you proofread your own writing. I'm giving you this kind of assignment because I believe there is some value for you, and for me, as your teacher, in seeing what you can do in one class period." I stop short of telling the boys this was a Dragon assignment, but they may sense that, given how quiet the room suddenly turns after my comments about finishing this in class.

Yet some of the boys accept this, albeit somewhat grudgingly, and begin to write. I wait my usual fifteen minutes again, this time more easily. When it's time to check on each boy, I see that most haven't generated any content, probably because I've skipped the usual discussion time to generate ideas. We didn't do that at the Dragon because the school respects the privacy of each child's thinking; Dragon kids don't share their work until they've completed an assignment, and their teachers rarely remark on a child's ideas in class unless those ideas are rude or unkind. I want to see if Fessenden kids can rise to this challenge of developing their own ideas without hearing from their peers. But, again, the assignment is too much for the majority of the class, so I give those who are stuck a suggestion for how to get started and step back to let them write.

What happens when some of us are asked to share our thoughts before each of us has a chance to develop our own? Do we influence or discourage others' ideas? Imagine being part of a committee working on a project together. Each of you has been asked to devise a solution to a problem. But if you know some of you are going to be asked to share your ideas before everyone is finished, haven't you eliminated the chance for each of you to take a risk? Some of you might even see this as an opportunity to dial back your thinking and be content to let others take the lead.

"Boys, there are twenty minutes left in the period. Don't worry too much about how or where to begin. Jump in and start from there. Take fifteen minutes to write, and then read aloud quietly to yourself to correct spelling, punctuation, and grammar. If you have a question, raise your hand, and I'll come over."

Their energy increases. I keep some distance to encourage independent work.

"Five minutes, boys. You should be reading your essays to yourselves to correct language errors."

Soon, fifteen papers scatter across my desk. The boys quickly put their books and belongings together and begin to leave the room.

I call out, "Thanks, boys, for giving this a try. I'm looking forward to reading your essays and will have them back to you on Monday. Homework is on the syllabus. Have a great weekend."

Monday morning, I return their work. My students have done

pretty well: four As, eight Bs, and three Cs. Very similar to my dragons' accomplishments. Not bad for their first attempt at an in-class
essay.

I hand them back and explain, "Boys, your essays have interesting
ideas and some good writing. We'll be writing an in-class essay each
week, so you'll have a chance to address problems one assignment at
a time and improve your writing. By the way, the letter grades you
received on these essays don't mean the same thing as they do on a
report card, where, for example, a B is the result of all your work for
the quarter or the semester. I use a system I learned at the Dragon.
A fourth of the class earns an A, half earns a B, and another fourth
earns a C. An A shows your essay is one of the best out of the fifteen
essays in the section. A grade of B indicates that it is quite good but
not in the top quarter of the class. C means it is not quite as good as
a B but shows some effort. Don't be too concerned about these letter
grades, because they can change with each assignment, depending
how well you do. Feel free to ask me any questions."

My students look over their papers, but no one has a question.
"Okay, boys, you can put your essays in the writing section of your
binder and take out the chart we started on concrete and abstract
nouns. It should be in the grammar section. Find a partner or two
and share what you have with each other so we all have the same
information."

I circulate and observe, "I can see from walking around that you
all have the same information now. Let's add some more nouns to the
chart; then we'll make a game with them."

I've re-created the chart on the whiteboard and ask two boys to
come up and write the nouns the others call out in the correct col-
umns. We go through six boys to be scribes at the board when the
class period is almost over, but the other nine boys want to know

when they will be able to be scribes, so I allow them to gather at the board and finish the exercise. It feels silly to do this because it becomes more about the boys and less about what they're meant to learn, but I remember how important it is at Fessenden that every boy has a chance at every activity. Not so at the Dragon. My dragons didn't care about that sort of equality. They knew they would have a chance at something at some point, but it didn't have to be every time I involved kids in an activity.

Inclusivity can be a tricky thing in our postmodern world. Pressure to include everyone may cause us to make attempts at doing so even when it feels unrealistic or may defeat our good intentions. There is great value in stepping back to watch things evolve as they will. Whatever is missing will be revealed, often with clear indications of how to recalibrate the situation.

The next day, Tuesday, Tom Miller, one of the school's administrators, appears in my doorway with a grimace on his face. I smile and walk toward him, but before I can say anything, he's already in the center of my room, his posture like that of one of his middle-school football players: legs spread, arms folded across his chest. He asks, "Barbara, got a minute?"

"Sure. What's on your mind?"

"You obviously had a terrific experience teaching at the Dragon, and I'm sure it's an adjustment to come back to Fessenden, but I think it would be best for the boys if you taught and evaluated them in ways that are familiar to them."

"Tom, let's sit down." I gesture to the center of the room. While he realigns a couple of desks, I close the classroom door and continue, "I see that you have some concerns, but I'm not sure what you're trying to tell me."

Tom leans back in his chair and drums his fingers on the desktop.

Then he clears his throat, sits up, and says, "Some parents have called. They're upset about the way you graded the boys' most recent essays. They think you're teaching the kids in ways that aren't the way Fessenden teachers teach, or indeed even the way you used to teach here." Tom gazes around my classroom at some of the art posters on the walls and looks at me sympathetically. I turn my head away for a moment and then look back at him. Tom continues, "Barbara, I'm all for different approaches to teaching, but the boys have struggled with several assignments you taught at the Dragon, and I note there isn't any student work on your walls, as there would have been in years past." He's right, but that's because the boys are still working on some pieces. As I did at the Dragon, I publish only work that reflects my students' best efforts. However, I don't share this thought, as it might create an argument between Tom and me.

Tom crosses his legs and twiddles his thumbs. "Before you went to England, you had developed a demanding but doable curriculum for the boys. Your graphic organizers helped them formulate ideas, and your rubrics kept the boys accountable. What you're doing now seems less supportive."

Tom also acknowledges how much I enjoy teaching the curricula I used at the Dragon, as well as some of its methodology, but he reminds me that Fessenden boys are not Dragon boys and that the Dragon's curriculum is not Fessenden's curriculum. "Here, students and their parents need to see you're the same challenging but flexible and empathic teacher you were before you left. I think it will be best for all concerned if you return to the methods and materials you used before going overseas."

What does Tom mean by his phrase "best for all concerned"? Is this about parents, kids, the school, me, or all of that? I don't want our conversations to become difficult, and, despite his gruff tone when he came in a few minutes ago, Tom has shown some sympathy toward me and my situation. So I err on the side of caution and agree with him, to a point: "Tom, you're right. Students at Fessenden and the Dragon *are* different, as are the curricula and the teaching methods at both schools. But that's partly why I took this exchange. I needed to grow personally and professionally. The experience has changed me, and, to a certain degree, I'm not the same teacher I was in 1997." I bite my lower lip.

Tom glances around the room. When he knows what he wants to say, he makes eye contact, but right now he seems at a loss for words. He stands, and I do the same. Together we push the desks back into place and walk to the door. Then he offers, "Let's touch base regularly to chat about how things are going. I'd be happy to teach a class for you sometime if you need a break."

Putting on my game face, I smile and say, "Sure! Thanks, Tom." He grins, opens the door, gives me a quick wave, and walks down the hall toward his office.

I wonder, *What did he have in mind, suggesting that he teach a class for me? Is that supposed to remind me how to teach at Fessenden? Oh well—maybe nothing will come of this. He sometimes doesn't follow up on things because he's forgotten, he's too busy, or he doesn't see the need.*

The one-thirty bell jolts me back to reality.

"Shit. I have a class," I exclaim. *Thank goodness my door is shut.*

I need to pull it together. Fortunately, this is my honors group; they're more independent. I'll give the boys a ten-minute freewriting period.

While the boys wrote, I make up discussion groups for *The Old Man and The Sea* and put them on the board. After a freewrite, the boys get into their groups. They know the drill: read ten pages aloud and come up with some topics to discuss. Someone in each group takes notes on their discussions and hands those to me at the end of class. I also give them, and myself, a break: no homework tonight.

The boys engage enthusiastically with the text and one another. Class is over sooner than I realize. Once the boys are out of the room, Tom's comments blast back into my brain. Despite the success of my last class, I wander around my classroom, rearranging furniture, posters on the walls, anything to create a sense of place for myself. Why is it so hard to realign myself with Fessenden? I plop myself down in one of the comfy reading chairs the boys like to use. Then I realize that Tom's offer to teach a class for me ticks me off. I feel as if I've just started my career and need the basic guidance I've given new teachers here as their mentor. I reach for one of the Sierra Club magazines on a nearby bookshelf and thumb through it. A photo of a mother bear and her cubs reminds me of Tom's care for the boys and his tendency to be too protective of them. Perhaps he's trying to be like a mother bear with me. He may see me, just back from the exchange, as a vulnerable cub right now. Maybe he wants to protect me from difficult moments with parents; perhaps his offer to teach a class for me was a genuine desire to help me transition back into what he can see is a very difficult situation for me.

It's hard to look past a person's initial actions or words when we feel vulnerable or annoyed. We get stuck in that place and can't imagine the other person has something helpful to say. Yet, despite such difficult experiences with our colleagues or friends, we can find great value in looking past this uncomfortable moment. By offering the benefit of the doubt, we recognize good intentions in language that initially felt hurtful or confusing. And ultimately, we can't know if this person might have second thoughts about what they said, and perhaps later, with another person, will offer more supportive comments.

We may not see or experience it ourselves, but it's my own belief that our life here is like a tapestry, in which we and God are the weavers. We can't see what God is weaving because God works in the front of the tapestry, and for now we are able to weave only from the back of it. (Fr. Martin Smith presented this idea in a webinar called "Deepening Prayer in a Time of Pandemic and Social Unrest," July 12, 2020.) However, a nonbeliever might view this tapestry image differently; by exercising mindfulness, she may "weave" present moments of her life together by paying careful attention to the feelings and thoughts that arise during her practice.

Chapter 10
Unexpected Gifts

B rady and I are in Montclair, New Jersey, my hometown, where we are spending Thanksgiving with my family. Time with them in such dear surroundings reminds me of how I spent Thanksgiving last year in Oxford. True, my Dragon colleagues made my heart merry with their chicken dinner and cranberry jam, but I feel just as blessed sitting around my parents' Thanksgiving table with my husband and my brother and his family. We all live so far apart now—my brother and his family in Ohio, Brady and I in Massachusetts, Mom and Dad in New Jersey—yet when we are together, we just pick up where we left off. The same routines resurrect themselves, especially at the dinner table.

"Okay, everyone. Let's all take a seat," Mom calls from the dining room.

We all trot in and sit in our appointed seats, marked by place cards. My dad, standing at the head of the table, puts down his carving knife, bows his head, and says grace. That done, we pass around plates, filling them with food as they go from one person to the next. The noise and antics begin.

"I don't want any turnips," my niece shouts.

"Watch out—you're spilling gravy all over the table," my dad calls out.

"Only take what you can eat," my sister-in-law reminds her daughter.

My brother gets up from the table to serve each of us mashed potatoes. He makes his way around the table. When he reaches my dad, spoon in midair, filled with potatoes, he begins to slowly lower the spoon down to my dad's plate. The potatoes edge themselves off the spoon, and then my dad does it: He whips his plate away, and the potatoes splat all over the table.

"Bill Kennard!" My mother laughs. "We never know when you're going to pull this trick, even though you've been doing it *forever*!"

My dad beams. "That's the fun of it. Just like being back in college!"

"Some people never grow up!" I joke. We all laugh. Dad scoops the splattered potatoes onto his plate and cleans off the table. We settle into more mundane topics of conversation: the weather, football, who wants to take a walk after dinner. The room fills with joyful noise.

Our feast finished, we clatter about the kitchen, cleaning up and reminiscing about past Thanksgivings with grandparents who are long gone. In this moment, I recall my English Thanksgiving in Jenny's little flat only one year ago. Even now, I can taste her roast chicken and, of course, the cranberry jam she was so apologetic about yet so "chuffed" to offer me. Here with my family and our Thanksgiving traditions, I am grateful for both ways of celebrating. Yet the differences between the two highlight what really matters about giving thanks: We are all, whatever our culture or condition in life, wired to express gratitude, and since we all do so differently, it hardly matters how we do it. What is paramount is our human need to give and receive thanks.

Tuesday, November 30, I return to school for three weeks of teaching. At morning meeting, everyone exudes energy and enthusiasm. We've all had a good rest, good food, and good times. This anticipation, this sense of something new, reminds me how much I love these weeks between American Thanksgiving and Christmas vacations: no tests or major assessments, no changes in the daily schedule, no after-school meetings, just teaching and learning. I like to do something students can really dive into during this time.

The boys begin a winter poetry unit I designed a few years before my exchange, though each year I switch some of the poems to make it new for them and for me. This year, I tweak the unit by adding three poems from my Dragon School collection of verse; however, I don't identity them as such.

Deep into our poetry unit, our first snow falls in a thick carpet on the soccer field outside my classroom.

"Boys, look, it's snowing." I exclaim, putting on my coat.

They get my idea and bundle up. After a quick "these are the rules outside" lecture, we head out to smell, breathe, taste, and touch the snow and to write more poems. But, instead of poems, fifteen angel shapes appear all across the soccer field.

"C'mon, Mrs. Kennard, make a snow angel with us!" the boys squeal.

"Sorry, but I'm not dressed for it, and neither are you. I didn't realize how messy it is out here. We'll write poems about being outside in the snow inside the classroom."

But they don't hear me. They're having too much fun jumping about in their jackets and ties, so I let them play for a few more minutes, until I see some teachers looking out the window at us. Do they think I'm irresponsible for letting my students outside?

"Boys, it's really cold. We're going inside for the rest of class." Most of them come along with me, but a few need reminders. At the door, I call out, "Josh, Ben, Craig, and Joey! It's time to come in!" They race past me into the building.

Dripping wet inside the classroom, they remove their jackets and rearrange their desks to create writing spaces of their own. They add an extra chair for me. For the rest of the period, we work on our poems in silence, and I remember from years past and at the Dragon how much it helped my students to see me write when they do. Typically, I need a solitary space and time, separate from my work as a teacher, to do my own writing. However, that isn't the point right now. The boys and I are settling in together, and something is happening in this moment between us. I can't say what it is, but I do know that I had this same feeling as a child when I sat with my family in the living room at night after dinner. We each had something to do—my dad with his paper, my mom with her needlepoint, my brother with his book, and I with my journal. There was no talking and no television. Just restful, working silence. A kind of holy silence. All families, including a family of one, need times of silence—a time to allow something to occur: a deepening peace at the end of a long day, a chance to prioritize our busy lives, or a sense that something unexplainable is at work in our midst, simply because we take time to sit and to be.

The boys and I journey along. Periodically, I read some of my favorite winter poems to them, and one or two students bring in some of theirs to share. All of them seem to relish this opportunity to write their own poems. Even though most of them are not ready to read their work aloud, the poetry unit is a success. For the first time this year, I feel as if the boys and I are well and truly on the same path.

On December 11, the last week of school before winter vacation, some of the boys ask to read their poems in front of the class, and that gives me an idea. On the way back from lunch the next day, I see Tom and present the idea of having some of the boys read their winter poems at the upcoming holiday assembly. Tom agrees but wants only one boy from each of my four sections to participate. I wonder if other students and maybe their parents will think these four kids have been singled out for special treatment, but I must get on and not let these worries get in the way of the boys' presentations.

As we approach his office, Tom's next comment catches me off guard: "By the way, Barbara, you must have made some changes in your teaching, as I suggested, because I haven't heard anything more from parents about your 'Dragon ways' with the boys," he declares, grinning.

I look at him without any expression on my face. As some boys walk by, I step away from them so we will not be overheard. Tom takes my cue and does the same. Then I divulge, "Yes, I've tried to do less of that, and the boys seem more at ease. When you and I talked, I think I was still feeling as if I was in two different schools at the same time, and although I appreciate some of the Dragon approaches to education, I also understand that some of these are unusual for the boys, though, to my surprise, they have asked from time to time to be told where they stand in the class. So I let them decide when they want to know that. Giving them the option seems meaningful to them, and they don't ask very often."

Tom smiles from ear to ear. "Good to know, Barbara. It seems like you've made the adjustment to being back here."

"Well, I think I'm in the process of doing that," I say.

He gives me a thumbs-up as he steps into his office. I head to my classroom, feeling good about our interaction.

Later that week in each of my classes, I ask for volunteers to read their winter poems at the holiday assembly. The response is better than I expected. Four or five boys from each section raise their hands. I tell Tom about their positive responses and ask if more kids can read. He agrees. Then he says, "I'm happy to accommodate them."

There's a moment of silence before he speaks again: "I'm glad your poetry unit has been successful. By the way, I saw you all out there in the snow last week."

I smile. "Oh, right! Yes, the boys were inspired to write poems by our quick trip outside." We both head off in different directions. Back in my classroom. I ponder Tom's comment about seeing the boys in the snow. Was he trying to tell me that he approved, or that I shouldn't have done it? It's not always clear what Tom means, but now, after my time at the Dragon, I decide I don't need to stress out about it. I remind myself to trust my intuition. And so, for us all. It's not only okay, but vital, that we give ourselves permission to lean on our own sense of what feels right and not spend time worrying about what others might think.

December 15. The last day of school before winter vacation and the day of the holiday assembly. Everyone gathers in Cahners Auditorium, and there is plenty of revelry. The place is decorated with a giant Santa Claus balloon, some reindeer, and a huge Christmas tree the kindergarten kids have decorated with paper ornaments. Kids and teachers converse about vacation plans. "Jingle Bells" plays in the background. I miss singing Christmas hymns, as we did at the Dragon, like "Silent Night" or "O Come, O Come, Emmanuel." So it is much to my surprise and delight that I discover that some of my students have written poems about their Christian faith and why this season is so meaningful to them. As each of them reads, I can tell from their confident, relaxed demeanor that they're enjoying the experience. I'm so proud of them. I'm glad I asked Tom if we could add more boys to the program. I also appreciate that they are the last to perform in the assembly, because we should all leave with poetry in our ears.

Traditionally after the assembly on this half day of school, the boys may choose to put holiday cards or gifts for their teachers in their classrooms and go home, while the adults gather in our dingy but cozy faculty room for coffee and pastries. As I'm pouring myself a cup of coffee, Mandy approaches me. "Great job with the poetry, Barbara. The boys did a terrific job explaining the unit and what inspired them to write their poems."

Ellie walks over and chimes in, "They were so courageous and self-assured."

"Thank you for your kind words. I'm very pleased for them," I say.

Mandy steps a little closer to me and asks quietly, "How did you get them to do this on their own? My students always want me to introduce them whenever they speak in an assembly. Sometimes they even want me to stand up there with them!"

I smile. "Actually, they wanted me to introduce them too, but I told them that if they wanted to read, they had to introduce themselves. I think they did well because they practiced together yesterday and this morning without me."

"That makes a lot of sense," Ellie says as she puts on her coat. "They probably also did well because they were in a group and not up there alone. I wish I could stay and chat more, but I have to pick up my kids at school. Have a wonderful holiday, and happy 2000!"

Mandy has to leave too. "Have a great vacation, and I look forward to trying out some of your strategies on my students."

"Happy holidays to you both!" I say as my two colleagues leave.

A few other teachers are still enjoying coffee. I wonder, *Should I chat with them or just go home?* My dilemma is solved as Saskia and Roberta approach me with smiles.

"Hey, Barbara. What gifts did you get from the boys?" Saskia asks. Before I can answer that I haven't been back to my room to look, she continues, "I am so amazed at the parents' generosity. One boy's family gave me four Red Sox tickets for next season! I'm not really a baseball fan, but I'll go because I could never afford to buy these. Besides, my husband will be psyched."

Then Roberta adds, "And I got an Hermès scarf. I can't wait to wear it to the Boston Pops' holiday concert."

As much as I want to say something nice, what comes out of my mouth is "Gifts? Oh my goodness, I forgot all about gift giving at Fessenden. It seems so strange to me now. It would have been unthinkable for a Dragon student to give a teacher a present. It could suggest a friendship between the child and the teacher, or inhibit teachers from evaluating student work honestly. I haven't been back to my room to get my things, so I don't know if I've received any presents." Before I even finish my words, I know from Saskia's and Roberta's glares that I've been too honest. A bit too English, perhaps.

"What a silly idea not to give teachers presents at Christmas. It's such a nice way to thank teachers for all their hard work. I can't believe you think it's strange," Saskia quips.

"I can't believe you didn't miss getting gifts. You used to get some really nice ones!" Roberta reminds me.

"Yes, I did in the past, but I didn't miss them at the Dragon last year, probably because by Christmastime I had made a pretty good adjustment to the school's way of doing things. When everyone around you is doing the same thing, you tend to join in, even if it feels different and strange."

"Why didn't you miss the presents?" Roberta asks, as if she might like to do without them herself.

"Well, to tell the truth, I often felt as if there might be strings attached to the gifts I received here in the past. It was nice not to worry about that at the Dragon."

Saskia jumps in: "Well, I don't agree, I don't think there are strings attached to teachers' presents. I think parents realize how hard we work and want to show their gratitude. It's none of my business if they choose to give me something expensive." With that, Saskia and Roberta pick up their coats and presents and prepare to leave.

I've put my foot in it. Saskia and Roberta are annoyed at my words and probably at the comparison I made between the two schools. They may feel as if I rubbed their noises in my experience at the Dragon. I also raised a bigger conundrum: Do families influence teachers' evaluations of their children with presents, or is gift giving just part of the culture here, the same way not doing so at the Dragon is part of its culture?

Stepping toward them in the doorway of the faculty room, I say, "Saskia, Roberta, I apologize if I said something that upset you. I guess I forgot how important it is to families here to give gifts and how much teachers appreciate them. I do remember that from past years. I hope you both have a wonderful vacation. Merry Christmas and happy New Year."

Saskia and Roberta stop in their tracks, with their coats half on. They look at each other and then at me. After an awkward silence, Roberta says, "You too, Barbara. Have a good holiday," and both of them leave the faculty room.

Back in my classroom, my interaction with Saskia and Roberta suddenly brings me to my knees. Instead of joining them in their excitement about their gifts, I judged them and a long-standing tradition at the school. While I'm personally uncomfortable with giving teachers gifts, a better response would have been something like "Saskia, that's so exciting to be going to a Red Sox game!" I may not like the Red Sox, or baseball, or even sports in general, but in that moment, it's not about what I like or don't like; it's an opportunity to appreciate and join in with her delight. What does it take for us to engage unselfishly with someone who is difficult, and what might we learn about ourselves when we take that leap? Indeed, people who irk us may well be our best teachers, because our response to them tells us a great deal about ourselves.

It's almost noon, and most of the classrooms are dark. I don't encounter anyone except one of the maintenance workers in the hallway on the way back to my room. We smile and exchange holiday greetings. My classroom lights are still on from the boys' rehearsal earlier this morning before the holiday program, the desks and chairs still assembled into a mock theater. I chuckle to myself that the boys went to all this effort to create an audience of chairs for themselves. Expecting kids to figure out some things on their own is one Dragon attribute that seems to work here at Fessenden.

As I'm preparing to leave, I look across my room and see several gifts and cards placed haphazardly on top of my bookshelf. Someone has given me a small arrangement of greens with red and white flowers and a gold candle in a wicker basket. Several envelopes lie scattered across a nearby desk, along with one other wrapped gift. I put the gifts and cards in my tote bag and carry the arrangement to my car.

Back home, I put some water in the greens arrangement and place it on our small dining room table, which Brady has set for lunch with my grandmother's linen tablecloth and red-and-green napkins.

Brady says of the arrangement, "That goes perfectly with our napkins! Who gave it to you?"

I pull a little card out of the flowers and read it: "Merry Christmas and happy 2000, Mrs. Kennard. With thanks from the Grangers."

Sitting down in a dining room chair, with Brady standing by my side, I open the other wrapped presents to find a floral-covered

journal from Craig and two gift cards for $25 each to Borders book-
store from Jason and Michael. Then I open the other cards, several of
which have quintessential sixth-grade boy messages:

*Thanks, Mrs. Kennard, for helping me when I had my con-
cussion this fall. I hope you have a merry Christmas. From
Tommy.*

*Hi Mrs. Kennard, have a fun holiday and don't eat too much
chocolate! Your student, Joe*

*Merry Christmas, Mrs. Kennard. My present to you is a pic-
ture I drew of you standing at the board teaching us grammar.
Jack*

Brady can see how choked up I am and hands me a glass of water.
"These are sweet messages, Barb."

"They are dear," I say, and take a sip of water. "I especially love
the simplicity of their messages. Like some of the notes my dragons wrote me when I left last summer. Those dragons gave me their
hearts. I think it's true what Jenny, my mentor, told me when I left.
She said, 'Barbara, you'll always be an old dragon.' And Jacqui made
a comment about how the English feel about people they like: 'Once
you are in our hearts, you are there forever.' I thought that by now
I'd be in better shape, since things are better at school, but I do miss
my dragons and all the people and places in England I love. They are
in my heart forever," I add, wiping a couple of tears from my cheek.

Brady sits and tries to help. "I know you still miss them, and you
probably will for some time, but tell me, how were the poetry reading
and the faculty coffee?"

I describe the terrific job the boys did at the assembly and the positive comments some of my colleagues made. But I also disclose my difficult interaction with Saskia and Roberta at the faculty coffee. "It was such an unpleasant moment; I wish I'd kept my mouth shut about the whole gift-giving scenario at Fessenden."

As he goes into the kitchen to bring in lunch, Brady reminds me that at least I had the insight to see I had upset my two colleagues. Coming back with a delicious lunch, he encourages me to feel good about my positive interactions with other teachers and adds, "Remember when you got upset with some of the unpleasant things that happened at the Dragon, like the turd incident? You handled that well, and you're doing same at Fessenden. Don't waste your energy on negative stuff."

As I consume a bowl of soup, I consider my husband's words. I know he's right, but instead of moving on, I describe my disappointment that Tom didn't acknowledge the boys' excellence. "It's not for me that I wanted him to remark on the readings; it's for the boys. They took a risk, and I wish he'd acknowledged that."

Brady asks, "Is it possible Tom said something to the boys when you weren't there to hear him?"

"I don't know; he was in such a hurry to leave after the assembly."

We seesaw: Brady wonders if it's really the case that I just want acknowledgment for the boys; I insist that's all I care about. He suggests I want something else from Tom. I remind him I got what I wanted. Brady must sense this too. After a moment of silence between us, he clears his throat and declares, "Barb, I think you're tying up your success with that of your students. That's natural to do, but you seem quite upset that Tom didn't say anything to you about the boys' success, and you equate your success with theirs and whether or not Tom recognizes that. You're forgetting that Tom has already remarked on your adjustments and success, but you're still not satisfied."

I stare out the window at our frost-covered shrubs. The dining room grows quiet. Brady works on his salad and asks, "Have I upset you?"

"Not really," I admit. "You're so gentle with your admonitions. What I hear you saying is probably true: I still have this tendency to seek perfection in my work. A bit of me thinks the whole is not good enough if some part is not attended to. In fact, what the boys accomplished was terrific, and I'm very happy they did it without me. You may be right about Tom saying something to the boys. He isn't easy to figure out, and I'm a bit out of practice with such things after having been at the Dragon, where the administrators were so up front about everything. But enough about them—I need to stop expecting so much from people and from myself. I want to give myself and others the benefit of the doubt and trust that we try our best, even if I'm unhappy with some aspect of it."

Brady pours each of us a bit more wine and raises his glass. "I'm so proud of who you are and your willingness to struggle through these moments. Here's to you!"

Picking up my glass, I sniffle and manage to respond, "Thank you. I think I'm coming around to accepting that my struggle with perfectionism is a lifelong one." We clink our glasses. Then I add, "If I can embrace it, then it may not be such a burden, especially if I can hand it over to God and see it as the path I've been given to become the person I am meant to be."

"Well and truly said!" Brady reaches for my hand across the table.

"Thank you for the part you play in all this and for your patience. You are such a gift to me," I say as I squeeze his hand.

"And you do the same for me. Never forget that we're a team. We don't figure this out alone or even as a couple. God already knows what we need, and together we are to be guided by the Holy Spirit. Now, speaking of gifts, let's put school away and talk about Christmas," Brady says, as he finishes his soup.

Chapter 11
New Millennium, New Job

January 12, 2000. The new millennium is under way!

With all the leisure of a free afternoon in mid-January, I put on a Bach CD, begin to put my classroom in order, and organize myself for the next day.

"Hi, Barbara. Sorry to disturb you," Tom Miller says as he enters my classroom.

I smile and say, "That's okay. What's up?" although I'm also thinking, *Oh, brother, I wonder what he wants now.*

"Barbara, I was impressed with your students' poems at the holiday assembly, so I'd like you to teach a creative writing class starting in February, using the new word processors we've purchased. It will mean four extra classes a week, but we'll pay you for it."

"Gosh, Tom, I'm not that confident with all this new technology." What an enigma he is. Not long ago, he suggested he teach a class for me! I want to think his compliment about my boys' poetry readings is genuine, yet he's tacked on a request for me to teach another class, on top of my full load. However, I do think he values my efforts to adapt to "the Fessy way," as he implied when he complimented me a while ago for dropping my Dragon lessons in favor of teaching what I've always taught here. He grasped that I was having a hard time readjusting to what is expected at Fessenden. Maybe asking me to teach this writing class is Tom's way of showing his faith in me; he could have asked another teacher to take it on, but he didn't.

Tom loosens his tie and clears his throat loudly. "Barbara, you had a bit of a rocky start to the year, but you seem to be in a better place now. Your students seem happier, and the parents are too. At the holiday assembly, a couple of moms commented to me about how much you're helping the boys with their writing. And don't worry about learning the technology—you can ask our new computer science teacher for help."

I smile broadly at Tom's remarks, but my insides are all scrambled: *Will some colleagues be unhappy about what may look like more favoritism toward me?* I can't know for certain. Although Tom communicates the mandatory nature of his requests with the words "I'd like you to . . . ," this could be a great opportunity to learn some technology and a new way for students to hone their writing skills. Technology is here to stay, and I may as well get onboard with it. I take a deep breath and tell him, "Okay. I'll give it a go."

"Great! You can design the class any way you wish. Thanks for your flexibility," he says, and almost skips out of my room.

My creative writing class takes off like a rocket. The boys love the freedom of writing and reading their work in class without receiving a grade. As much as I enjoy the class, planning new assignments and losing my lunch hour several days each week exhausts me. Soon after we commence this class, Tom asks me to incorporate some of the material from the boys' science, social studies, and geography classes. That solves the problem of designing new material, but Tom wants me to meet with the teachers of these other classes to build a cross-curricular program. I wish I'd seen this coming and had had the courage to say no to the class. The English poet W. H. Auden sure got it right when he wrote, "Nothing fails like success." I must make some decisions about my workload; my moment comes in mid-February, the time when contracts for the coming school year are discussed.

"Knock, knock, Barbara. May I come in?" Fred Post asks, leaning against the doorway of my room.

"Hi, Fred. Yes, do come in." I put down an eraser to shake his hand.

"Barbara, we are so lucky to have you back at Fessenden, and I know how hard the transition returning from the Dragon has been for you, but I hope things are better now and that you will accept this contract for the 2000–2001 school year," he says as he hands me a thick packet.

I smile and take the packet from his hand. "Thank you, Fred. Things *are* better. But I would like to discuss my workload for next year. I need to drop the writing class that was added this semester, one of the English classes I teach, or the fall coaching season. I don't have time for lunch on Mondays and Thursdays, and the extra work leaves me little time to mentor our new teacher, Mandy." I hope he doesn't sense how anxious I feel about asserting myself. I run my fingers across the raised seal on the envelope to regain my composure.

Fred puts his hands in his pockets and shifts his feet apart. "I'll speak to Tom. You have to have lunch every day, so we'll work that out, but I can't promise any other changes. We want to stay on the growing edge of technology with this writing class. You're doing a great job with the boys; they love it. And, as you know, all faculty must coach a sport at least two of the three seasons."

Now, I work my fingers harder over that raised seal as I reply, "I'm willing to drop the fall coaching and take a cut in my salary, if need be. We don't have as many players at that time of the year. I would be of better use in the spring, when we have forty kids on the team."

Fred furrows his brow. "We can't make exceptions for the coaching.

Every faculty member signs on for this. It's the only way we can have a good competitive sports program."

"But I coach an intramural team. We aren't competitive except within the team."

"Technically, intramural tennis *is* competitive because you have matches with another school at the end of the season, which is a great opportunity for boys who are trying to make it onto the junior varsity team. I would hate to see that standard abandoned," Fred remarks, crossing his arms over his chest.

I'm not going to win on the coaching. Better to be happy that I'll get lunch every day. I put the packet down. "All right, Fred. I understand the school's position." We shake hands before he leaves.

Once Fred is out of the room, I return to my desk, stuff the packet in my briefcase, and consider my dilemma. I love certain aspects of my job. The boys have become a delight to teach, and I teach my passions: literature, grammar, drama, and writing. But the school won't negotiate anything related to the coaching part of my job. However, despite this conundrum, I think I have a pretty good situation at Fessenden, given the school's willingness to let me teach overseas for a year, so I'm going to make the best of the situation and sign my contract for next year.

Then, just when I thought things were settling down, I receive this email.

Hi Barbara,

Welcome back from England!

I hope you remember me; in 1997–'98, the year before you went on exchange, I was a math intern at Fessenden. You helped me a lot during that training year, and now I'm teaching math at NCDS (Newton Country Day School).

There's an opening here for an English teacher for next year.
I think you'd be great for the job. If you're interested, let me
know, and I'll tell the headmistress about you.
    Sincerely,
    David Donnelly

Where did this come from? Out of the blue . . . or by the hand of God? What's God weaving into the tapestry of my life?

My imagination runs wild as I begin to stack up reasons to take this opportunity. At a new school, I wouldn't have the sense that I don't fit in. And, best of all, I could teach girls! I attended an all-girls school from fifth through twelfth grade and loved it. Teaching girls would give me an opportunity to give back what some of my teachers at the Beard School for Girls gave to me: confidence in myself and a love of learning.

Then my conscience enters in: *On the other hand, Fessenden has been really good to me, and things are improving here for me. With another year after this one, I might feel like more a part of the community again.*

But boys can be so immature at this age. Some middle-school boys aren't ready for serious work; they're too busy roughhousing in the hallways and picking their noses in class, and they forget everything. Girls are definitely more mature in middle school.

On the other hand, I have just signed and turned in my contract.

Never mind that. It's still early in the year. There are usually lots of teachers still looking for jobs in February, and even in March and April. The school will surely find a replacement for me.

But I did something like this in 1997, when I was a finalist for a job at the Winsor School. I kept asking for a delay in returning my contract because Winsor needed more time to make its decision.

Yes, and Fessenden gave me until May to sign. I have time to explore this. I should at least tell David I'm interested in knowing more and see what happens after he talks to the headmistress.

After emailing with David to learn more about the school and the position, I send in my résumé. Since I'm in the early stages of the application process, private-school protocol doesn't require me to tell Fessenden that I'm applying for another job; that obligation comes when a teacher is a finalist for a position.

During spring break in March, I have a wonderful interview with Marian Roberts, the headmistress of NCDS, and Teresa Connelly, the assistant head. After we exchange the usual niceties, Marian asks me, "What draws you to a girls' independent Catholic school?"

I've been hoping for this question since my Winsor experience didn't pan out. Although I'm not Catholic, I hope my Anglican sensibilities will fit in some way with this school. Pulling myself forward in the comfy sofa I'm sitting in, I look Marian in the eye and declare, "I attended the Beard School for Girls in New Jersey from fifth through twelfth grade. I had wonderful teachers, several who had and continue to have an impact on my life. I'd like a chance to give back to girls what my teachers gave to me."

Marian and Theresa smile at each other, and then Teresa says, "Tell us about one of your teachers."

I grin and describe Mrs. Church. "She was my seventh-grade English teacher, and I loved hearing her talk about books such as *Jane Eyre*. She was funny and kind but also very serious. I was your typical seventh-grade girl—too social, too anxious about anything and everything, and definitely boy crazy—but Mrs. Church's quiet strength inspired me to buckle down and develop my skills as a reader and writer."

Theresa acknowledges, "Sounds like you know seventh-grade girls pretty well, even though you've been teaching sixth-grade boys."

I'm on a roll and reply, "One of my quintessential memories of seventh grade is the locker room and all that goes on there: rounds of gossip, last-minute hairstyles before class, and the ultimate tragedy of not being able to open one's locker."

Marian says, "Oh, we have lots of that here!"

The three of us continue to reminisce about our own experiences in school, and then Marian tells me, "We're narrowing down the pool of candidates for the seventh-grade English job. We'll be asking finalists to come back and teach a class, spend time with the English-department teachers, and have lunch with the search committee and other colleagues. It's usually a pretty full day. If you're a finalist, will you be able to do this?"

I pause for a minute and then say, "Of course. That wouldn't be a problem at all."

Marian stands; Theresa and I do the same. Marian then leads us to her office door. Before she opens it, she smiles and, glancing at Theresa, who is also smiling at me, says, "Thank you, Barbara, for coming in. We've enjoyed chatting with you and very much appreciate your experience and your reasons for wanting to teach in a girls' school. You obviously have a great deal to offer. My assistant will call you if you end up a finalist." And, with a twinkle in her eye, Marian shakes my hand and opens the door for me.

I thank them both and make my way to the parking lot in the back of the school building. I put on some quiet classical music for the drive home, relishing my interactions with these two women, who, with their humor and forthrightness, coincidentally remind me of my Beard School teachers.

A week later I receive an invitation to teach a class, meet with the search committee, and have lunch with the English department.

On a bright day in early April, I arrive at NCDS to teach a history section of seventh-grade girls. Since they're learning about the apartheid system in South Africa, I decide to introduce them to the book *The Boy Child Is Dying*, by Judy Boppell Peace. I rearrange the rows of desk chairs into a circle and sit with the girls. I show them the book and tell them it was written by my friend Judy, who lived in South Africa during some of the worst years of apartheid. The girls sit up and look intently at me as I explain, "I'll read the first chapter to you. It's short but a good introduction to the book. As I read, think about the apartheid system you're learning about in your history class and try to make some connections to what you hear me describing."

When I finish reading, the room is quiet. The girls look at each other and then at me. I pass the book around. For a few minutes, they each look intently at the book's cover illustration, of a young African boy and his mother. Then the room fills with what I call thinking noise, and when it looks like everyone might have something to offer, I ask, "Would one of you like to share a connection?"

No one raises her hand. I'm starting to sweat. To boot, the search committee is watching me and furiously writing down notes. I look at the girls and wait. It always feels like an eternity whenever I do this with students, but I hold my ground and then it happens. Samantha raises her hand and says, "We've been learning about how it was illegal in South Africa during apartheid for Black people to work alongside whites, so I was totally shocked at the way the white woman and the Black woman in this story were working together as equals. I really loved the way they each could speak honestly to each other about working together."

The girls look at each other, fidget with their ponytails, and adjust themselves in their chairs. The search committee has stopped writing. I thank Samantha for getting us started and look to the other girls. Suddenly, the room fills with conversation, and I wonder if we'll even get to the poetry-writing part of my lesson plan, which I wrote on the board before class started, but I let the girls carry on with their discussion. When their conversation begins to die down, I say, "Your insights and ideas about this first chapter are so interesting, and I think we all appreciate that everyone contributed to the conversation. I understand you've been writing poems in your English class; I'd love to see you each write a poem about something in this chapter that really resonates with you."

The room fills with my favorite noises: Desktops creak open, binders click, paper shuffles, pencils are sharpened, and the girls settle down to writing. I write too. Toward the end of the period, two search committee members come up to thank me profusely and excuse themselves politely for another commitment. A little while later, I check the clock on the wall, and although I'd like the girls to read their poems, it's time for class to end. "Girls, it's been a real plea-sure to be with you today. Thanks for all your efforts and your ideas. I hope you will keep writing poems!" I collect their work as they gather their books. Individually and in pairs, they make their way to the door, most of them stopping on the way to thank me, to ask me more about the book, or to wish me good luck with the interview process. Their teacher approaches me; as I give her the girls' poems, she says, "Thank you so much, Barbara. I really enjoyed your lesson. I think I'll add poetry writing to my syllabus from time to time!"

After all my responsibilities conclude, I offer my thanks to everyone and return to the faculty room. While I'm collecting my belongings, Julie, one of the search committee members, pops in to say, "Barbara, Theresa Connelly asked me to bring you to her office to say goodbye."

Julie and I walk through quiet, carpeted halls; one or two school-girls smile and say hello as they pass us. Julie knocks on Theresa's door and opens it. "Theresa, here's Barbara Kennard," Julie says, and pats me on the back as she leaves.

Closing her office door, Theresa offers me a seat on a pink over-stuffed couch. "Barbara, thank you for coming in today. I've heard from several teachers that your day went very well. How did it feel to you?"

"I had a wonderful time introducing the girls to a South African story. I wish I didn't have to leave, but I have to get back to Fessenden to teach a class at two o'clock."

Theresa smiles, rises from her chair, and approaches me with her hand extended. I stand and offer mine.

"Barbara, you only have to leave for now, if you wish. Many of the teachers who observed your teaching or spoke with you today were very impressed with your lesson and the way it engaged all the girls. Marian Roberts is away today, but I have spoken with her by phone, and she has given me the authority to offer you the position."

I can hardly breathe but manage to come out with "Oh my goodness, thank you! I am really pleased, but before I officially accept it, I think I should tell my principal, which I can't do until tomorrow."

It doesn't occur to me to ask for some time to think about it, to discuss it with Brady, and, most importantly, to pray about it. On the other hand, I don't need to deliberate too hard. I've wanted this kind of job for so long, and now it's here. I don't understand how such things work, but I'll trust God's hand in this.

"Certainly. In fact, Marian won't be back until tomorrow as well. And she'll want to ask Fred Post for a recommendation. Pending a good reference, which I am sure he will give you, she'll call to confirm the offer and review our compensation package with you."

I float out of Teresa's office, down the wooden staircase, and through the front door to drive back to Fessenden, miraculously avoiding an accident.

Back at Fessy, I come to terms with what I have to do. I need a reference from Fred *after* I've signed my Fessenden contract? How on Earth do I do *that*?

After my last class, which I teach in a complete daze, I make my way to Fred's office and ask his administrative assistant if I can see him for a few minutes before the end of the day. She looks at his calendar and says she isn't sure he has time to see me.

My legs are shaking as I stand in front of her desk and say, "I know he's busy, but I need to talk to him this afternoon. It's about next year." The phrase "it's about next year" is language a teacher generally uses to communicate something important about the coming school year, such as that they aren't planning to return. I hope my words motivate Fred's assistant to get up, knock on his door, and tell him I have an urgent need to speak with him.

She gives me a blank look, thumbs through Fred's calendar, and checks another, bigger, all-school calendar on the wall behind her desk. She peers over her spectacles at me. Now I'm worried there are even more reasons besides his own calendar that Fred won't be able to see me. Then she informs me, "I just don't see a minute in his sched-ule when he can see you this afternoon. He hasn't even had lunch yet today. He could see you tomorrow at eight thirty or eleven o'clock."

Oh God, I don't know what to do. I hope Marian won't call before eight thirty. Maybe I should take that slot? I could also call NCDS and tell them Fred isn't available until after eight thirty. No, that would look weird, like I'm too anxious to get this job.

I take a deep breath and answer, "Okay, I'll take the eight-thirty time."

"I'll put you in for then. About how much time do you need with him?" she asks with a smile.

"Not a lot. Maybe ten or fifteen minutes." I feel a bit wobbly.

"Okay. He's tentatively scheduled for a meeting at eight fifty, so that works. Could I give him a sense of what you want to speak to him about?" She looks up at me expectantly with her pencil poised, ready to write whatever I say.

I swallow and stutter, "It's . . . it's about next year." I give her a certain look, as if to say, *I have another job! The head of the school is calling tomorrow to ask for a reference—that's why I need to see Fred today.*

"Okay, I'll put that on his memo for the meeting. And he'll know what that means?" she asks, without looking up from her appointment calendar.

I smile and reply, "Yes, I think he will."

The day is over. I can go home. I pack up student papers to grade tonight and look at my plan book to make sure everything is set for tomorrow. *Oh, crap! I can't believe it! What was I thinking? I have a class at eight thirty tomorrow morning. Now what do I do? Well, it's obvious, Barbara: You need to get yourself over to Fred's office and change the appointment to eleven o'clock, when you're free.*

I scurry out of my room, race down the hallway, and open the door to the hallway that leads to the administration offices. Walking as fast as I can, I round the corner and see Fred. He's coming toward me. Maybe he knows. Maybe Marian has already called him. No, that can't be. I told Teresa I needed time to tell Fred today. He's seen me; I can't turn around now.

"Barbara, hello!" Fred calls as he walks closer to me.

"Oh, hi, Fred." I barely get it out.

"You wanted to see me?" He has such a kind voice.

"Yes, I wanted to talk with you about next year," I say, in barely more than a squeak.

"Okay. I was on my way home, since my two-thirty meeting has been rescheduled. If it's not too complicated, why don't we talk now in your classroom?" He puts out his arm to indicate we can walk together.

What a gift! But I'm also sweating like a pig. Fred has caught me off guard, and he's got such a sweet smile on his face. I feel awful about what I'm going to do.

"Thank you, Fred. That would be great." We both walk toward my classroom.

As we pass through the hallway toward my room, I'm sure Fred can hear my heart pounding. Now I've gotten what I've asked for, and maybe in more ways than one. I have Fred's attention and, I hope, a new job.

But guilt sweeps over me. *I shouldn't do this. I shouldn't do this to someone who's given me a great deal of support. If I do this, it will seem like a slap in the face to Fred. I should stay here and work to make things even better next year.*

Really, Barbara? After the wonderful day you just had at NCDS, you could give up the chance to teach at a girls' school? You'd let go of a chance to make a difference in girls' lives, as your teachers did in yours?

No. No, I can't walk away from this opportunity. And I can talk with Fred about it. After all, I was able to talk at great length with him about Winsor, about the Dragon, and about my workload. Here goes!

At my classroom door, I take a deep breath and open it, saying, "Please, Fred, after you," as I gesture him into my room. I follow and close the door behind me and say, "Let's sit down," as I place two chairs across from each other.

Fred stares quizzically at the chairs and sits. For a moment, he looks like a doggie in training, and I have a sickly sense in my gut that he has no idea what I'm about to tell him, despite my use of the phrase "it's about next year." But I have to do this, so I sit. My arms straight and rigid, I must look like I'm about to rocket out of the chair. I take another breath and fold my hands in my lap.

Crossing his legs, Fred asks, "What's up, Barbara?'

I squirm in my seat and begin, "Fred, this is difficult news, but I want to tell you that I visited NCDS today for a job interview. Right after I signed my Fessy contact for next year, David Donnelly, the math intern here in 1997–'98, emailed me about an English job at NCDS. As you know from my application to Winsor, I would like very much to teach at a girls' school. Before I left NCDS today, the assistant head offered me the job and said the head of the school would call you tomorrow for a reference about me. I wanted to tell you myself before she calls." My heart pounds hard.

Fred smiles, his eyes a tad watery. "Barbara, I will be sad to see you go, but after the rejection from Winsor, it's rather nice that this opportunity to teach at a girls' school has come your way. Earlier this year, whenever I saw you in the hallways or at a meeting, you often looked sad. Perhaps a new school will help you miss the Dragon a little less. I look forward to Ms. Roberts's call. It will be my delight to recommend you with the highest regard," he says, and extends his hand.

He is so like those at the Dragon. I hold back tears and say, "Thank you, Fred. I am honored by your words. I will always be grateful for all you have done for me."

I shake his hand, after which he gives me a hug and pronounces, "You are a class act, Barbara."

"Thank you again!" I feel too emotional to say anything else without losing it. Fred stands to leave. I walk him to the door. We say goodbye at the same time, and I watch him walk out of the building, toward the faculty parking lot.

Alone in my room, I tear up over all the lovely things Fred has just said to me, and, given his words, I think maybe he did know, or at least had an inkling of, what I wanted to tell him. He and I may not have agreed about certain aspects of my workload, but he's never held that against me. He could have taken my news personally, but he didn't. Fred's a class act too.

On Friday evening, the day after I tell Fred about the NCDS job, Marian Roberts calls me at home to give me the news. "Barbara! I'm so glad to reach you on a Friday night! Can you talk right now?"

My heart skips a beat as I say, "Yes, of course," hoping my tone of voice doesn't sound too serious.

She tells me what a great recommendation Fred gave me, as well as her regard for him. "I know Fred, and he always plays it straight, so when he had such glowing things to say about your work at Fessenden, the impression I had of you at your initial interview was confirmed. You are the right candidate for this position." She reviews the compensation package with me, and I accept it. Before we say goodbye, she adds, "Barbara, I'm thrilled you'll be joining us. We've been waiting for a teacher like you for a long time."

I gather myself and quietly reply, "Thank you, Marian, for your kind words. I feel the same way—I've wanted to teach at a school like NCDS for a long time."

Monday morning, I give Fred the news and thank him for his recommendation.

"It was a pleasure, Barbara. We will be sorry to see you go, but this opportunity seems quite serendipitous, given all you've been through. Now we'll let the community know of your plans. First, I'll inform the faculty at our meeting this Thursday that you're moving on to a position at NCDS; then you can tell the boys in your classes on Friday."

After the announcement about my departure and that the school will be conducting a search for my replacement, Mandy and Ellie and a few other teachers congratulate me and tell me how much I will be missed. However, most of my colleagues have little to say about my news, perhaps because searching for a replacement for any teacher is difficult and time consuming, or maybe they just don't know what to say. Is it possible they aren't all that upset about my departure? Whatever the reason, I decide not to dwell on their silence or try to figure out the whys and wherefores of it.

Besides, the boys have such sweet things to say when I tell them. In typical sixth-grade language, they say, "You're a great teacher, even though you make us learn grammar" and, "We'll miss you a lot, but we hope you'll like your new job." Several boys are excited because their sisters go to NCDS, and say, "That would be so cool if you got to teach them."

After the school hires a young man to take my position, everyone's focus, including mine, switches to finishing the many tasks that need to be accomplished by early June.

Are there moments when I wonder if I'm doing the right thing? Not really, though I will miss certain people at and aspects of Fessenden: my colleagues who have been so supportive this year; the school's innovative approach to teaching boys to be compassionate, curious, and strong; Fred, for his deep respect and care; and even Tom—he means well, and I'm pleased we found a way to work together. Of course I'll miss my boys too, and will take many images of them with me, my favorites of which include watching them making snow angels in their jackets and ties, their reactions to eating M & M's as part of a lesson on transitive verbs, grumbling about revisions but doing them, and carrying on about how my homeroom was like a class because I made every boy show me that he had all his materials before going to class or going home.

Such is the way of departing. We take things with us, we leave parts of ourselves behind. The key to moving on is to do so with grace and goodwill, no matter why you're headed out the door. Most people don't remember what you said or how you looked or what you did or didn't accomplish. What we leave behind is how we made a difference in someone's life. I trust that I have done that as best I could here at Fessenden.

Chapter 12
And All Shall Be Well

June 8, the day of closing ceremonies, has arrived!

Beforehand, Tom addresses the middle-school faculty and students: "This has been another tremendous year in the middle school. I want to thank each and every one of you for your energy, dedication, and flexibility." He pauses and looks at me, his lower lip slightly aquiver, as he continues, "We will say goodbye to Barbara more formally in the all-school closing assembly, but I believe some students have something to say. George, would you come forward now?"

I'm not prepared for this! Surely it won't be like the Dragon kids' skits.

George, who is one of my advisees, and a few other boys come up to the front of the room, where we are all gathered in a semicircle of chairs.

The boys smile sheepishly at me. George takes out a piece of paper and begins to read a letter to me: "Dear Mrs. Kennard, you have been an excellent teacher and leader for us all. You really helped to guide us down the right path toward success. You discovered our talents and then helped us get better at them, and that's what we all ask for in a great teacher."

Michael continues, "Mrs. Kennard, you taught us many, many,

many things in English, like poems, semicolons, grammar, and all about Shakespeare."

Then Bobby: "You're a great teacher, Mrs. Kennard, you never fail at doing what is right for your students, and we'll miss you."

The boys give me a rousing sendoff. I recognize some sixth-grade voices hooting and whooping. Ben and Jonathan hand me some flowers and the letter, which the entire class has signed.

I put my hand to my heart and stand up. "Thank you, boys, for your funny and loving tribute to me. I will keep this letter forever, and all of you in my heart too."

After I sit down, the teachers applaud politely. Tom stands and looks at me while he fiddles with his tie. "Thank you, Barbara, for all your contributions to Fessenden. You have made such an important impact here with your dedication to teaching boys how to be good writers and readers, and you have contributed in many ways to our community outside the classroom as well. We will miss you and wish you all the best." As everyone claps politely, I get hold of myself. What a nice surprise to have Tom speak this way about me. I guess it just goes to show that we can never be sure how someone might feel about us and shouldn't assume that we know someone as well as we think we do.

On the way to Cahners Auditorium for the all-school meeting, some of my students run up to walk side by side with me. We chat a bit about summer vacation plans, and they want to know more about my new job. Their genuine enthusiasm and interest in me makes my eyes water. I see the ladies' room nearby and tell the boys, "You go ahead into the auditorium; I'll find you in a minute."

Once inside the bathroom, I settle myself with a drink of water and leave to find my students. We wait for Fred to appear at the podium. Finally, he arrives and launches into a complimentary speech to all the boys about memorable moments of the year, including sports awards and admissions for the ninth graders to high schools throughout New England. Next, he acknowledges three teachers who are each taking a leave of absence in the fall.

Then Fred's tone becomes more serious. "Despite all the many things we have to celebrate at the end of a school year, we sometimes have to say goodbye to people who are moving on from Fessenden. I want to say a few words about Barbara Kennard, who, as you all know, has accepted a position at NCDS.

"Barbara came to us seven years ago, in the fall of 1993. During her time here, she has led the way forward with some unique opportunities for the sixth grade. In her first two years, she inspired the boys to rousing performances of *A Midsummer Night's Dream* in the Memorial Garden, encouraging subsequent performances to be directed by the boys themselves. No student who has had Mrs. Kennard leaves her English class without a thorough understanding of the parts of speech! All our boys finish sixth grade with the ability to write clear sentence structure, and neither do they depart without an abiding love for such classic books as *The Old Man and the Sea*, *Of Mice and Men*, *The Adventures of Tom Sawyer*, and *Treasure Island*.

"Not one to be daunted by the onset of technology, Barbara agreed to teach a creative writing class with our new word processors. In collaboration with her sixth-grade colleagues, the boys wrote stories and poems based on curricula from their other classes.

"Barbara has given of herself outside the classroom too. She also helped to develop our delightful reading buddies program with the sixth-grade boys and the kindergarten. Barbara has served on our admissions and faculty compensation committees as well, and has mentored several interns. Barbara, we will miss your energy, competence, and creativity. Thank you for all you have given us. We wish you every success at NCDS. Please come forward to accept this gift as a token of our appreciation."

As I stand and make my way to Fred, the room fills with gracious but restrained applause. At the podium, Fred hands me a book on British writers, gives me a hug, and whispers, "I think great things await you at NCDS. Good luck."

I smile as I say, "Fred, you've been so supportive over these years. I will always be grateful for my time at Fessy."

Afterward, we all gather outside to wave goodbye to the boys as they stream off in station wagons for the summer. Mandy, Ellie, and I walk back to our classrooms. In the hallway, Ellie gives me a hug and a plant and says, "Good luck, Barbara. I will miss your laugh. Come back and visit."

After she leaves, Mandy takes out some flowers from behind his back and offers them to me. "Barbara, these flowers are a paltry thank-you gift for all the help you've given me as a new teacher this year."

"They're beautiful. Thank you! It's been a pleasure to teach with you, Mandy. I really appreciate all your invitations to have tea in the afternoons. Even if I couldn't always accept them, they meant a great deal to me. My best wishes to you."

After I say goodbye to Ellie and Mandy, I return to my room to retrieve a few boxes of books and other materials. On my desk lie a number of handwritten notes, mostly from parents and kids, and some from boys I taught two three or four years ago. A few teachers have also written me some words of goodbye, but, for the most part, my leaving seems to stir little sense of loss in my colleagues. One reason may have to do with the way private schools engender a strong sense of loyalty from their personnel, a sort of "you are part of a family, and you can't leave" mentality. Or perhaps some colleagues feel as if I'm being untrue to the school by leaving for something better after Fessenden gave me my exchange opportunity. Do they sense betrayal in my departure?

My colleagues' reaction to my departure recalls how very differently the Dragon folks said goodbye to me, with such warmth and goodwill, a year ago. As English people, they have a sense of duty to one another, and especially to visitors, that doesn't allow them to be anything other than gracious. It's part of their national identity. In contrast, we Americans have less and less of a sense of duty to others. Our addiction to a "free to be me" way of life has made many of us preoccupied with what is "fair" and "unfair" to our individual sensitivities, rather than what serves others for the good of all.

Yet a note from one Fessenden colleague helps me put all these thoughts in perspective:

> Dear Barbara,
>
> It has been a number of years now that we have been co-coaches in tennis; I am sad that you are leaving Fessenden and will miss your constancy. You are a fine teacher; NCDS is fortunate to be getting you, and we will be poorer for your leaving, but I am awfully excited for you, Barbara. It hasn't been easy for you to be back here after your successful year in England. I feel that you will be glad for this change and will love teaching girls!
>
> My best wishes for every success,
> Cindy Cosentino

I wonder if some of my coworkers feel the way Cindy does about my departure. Is their coolness a kind of relief for themselves and maybe even for me? It's not easy to be around someone who makes things happen for herself, especially if she's been a bit of a thorn in other people's sides. Goodness knows I've felt that way about colleagues at various schools over the course of my career. I think we all have those moments when we realize our feelings toward others might just be the same way they feel about us.

Even so, I know the Dragon would applaud my choice to move on to another institution. Of course, I would be missed, but the school would celebrate this opportunity for me to begin again. Indeed, while I was there, several teachers in various phases of their careers had secured positions at other schools, not only in England but across the globe. Moreover, the headmaster helped some of them find these new opportunities, not because he wanted them to leave but because the school considered working in a range of settings vital for a teacher's growth.

In my first few months back at Fessenden last fall, I felt as if I were starting from scratch in getting to know the ways of the school again—how it operates and how people there relate to one another. Yet, as I look back over this year, I understand something now that I never would have embraced before my experience at the Dragon: No matter how good a teacher I may be, I am and will always be a beginner because there will always be something new for me to learn about myself and my craft. And so it is for us all. We are always beginners. Each time we do something new, we are beginners, and when we complete something, we are still beginners, for "what we call the beginning is often the end and to make an end is to make a beginning. The end is where we start from" (T. S. Eliot, "Little Gidding," stanza five, in *Four Quartets*).

Epilogue

It's a bright and breezy day for mid-November in Oxford in 2018. Brady and I are here after a trip to Amsterdam, one of our bucket-list destinations. Flying in and out of London affords us the chance to visit old English haunts and friends. Twenty years after teaching all those dragons, I'm back, but this time as an old dragon. Last month, when searching the school's website, I wasn't able to find emails for Jenny, Debbie, and Betsy, so I contacted two other former colleagues, Pierre and Monica, to see if they could meet Brady and me for lunch while we're in Oxford. Pierre and Monica were not close friends of mine while I was at the Dragon, but we were more than acquaintances; Monica entertained us several times in her home, and Pierre and I chaperoned a number of fields trips together.

We're in the Rose and Crown on North Parade Road, waiting for Pierre and Monica to join us for a pub lunch. The dingy back room is exactly as I remember it from the few times I met friends here when I lived in Oxford. The long wooden tables are honed down to the grain. The same wobbly benches and a few chairs line the small, dark room, brightened by a screened-in porch and a few plants, the walls plastered with adverts for all kinds of drinks and drinkers who've frequented this place. An equally ragged board warns patrons of the wobbly steps into the dining area. This is the place where Dragon teachers retreated for drinks during or after a long day, though I was not one of them. I preferred to take tea with colleagues. Imagine one of Fessenden's teachers "nipping off to the pub" in the middle of the school day! But this is Pierre and Monica's favorite pub, and we're happy to meet them here. I look at the menu plastered to the wall detailing the food on offer: toad in the hole, shepherd's pie, fish and chips.

It's one thirty. Maybe Pierre and Monica are in some other part of the pub? We go inside to look for them. I investigate the back dining room. It's empty. But then I hear their voices in one of the smaller dining rooms to one side of the front door. They sound just like they did twenty years ago! I run into the room. My two former colleagues see me and exclaim, "Hey, Ma Kennard," hugging me. Pierre directs us to the table where they're sitting; a waiter comes over with menus.

While we dine, the four of us catch up on school news. I describe our visits in the summers of 2002 through 2005 to do house exchanges with former Dragon colleagues. Monica exclaims, "I heard about those house swaps! Must have been good fun for you to come back and for Dragon families to see Boston."

Monica adds that she retired in 2015 but still works part-time for the school in an administrative role. Pierre tells us how much he still enjoys taking Dragon students on trips. "I've been to all kinds of places with the children—parts of Africa, New Zealand, Japan, and Norway—though I don't manage the tours anymore. Younger staff do that."

After we get through more gossip about marriages, births, and divorces, I comment about the absence of Betsy's, Debbie's, and Jenny's names on the school website. "Jenny and I stayed in touch for a while after I returned to Fessenden in 1999, so I knew about her move to a school in Norfolk, but I also noticed that Debbie's and Betsy's names weren't listed as part of staff anymore."

Pierre explains, "Debbie returned to Scotland to be near her family, and Betsy retired a few years ago."

"Oh, right. I remember now: Debbie's parents live near Dundee. Is Jenny still in Norfolk?" I ask.

Pierre and Monica look at each other. Pierre grows quiet. Then he tells me the news: "Jenny died this past July after a long and courageous battle with breast cancer."

I am stunned silent. Pierre and Monica look at me with such compassion, I almost break down. Brady puts his arm around me. I manage to say, "I am so sorry. What terrible news. She was such a wonderful mentor to me all those years ago."

Monica sympathizes, "It is a great loss to us all. Jenny was a consummate teacher, and she gave unstintingly of herself right to the end of her life."

There is a sense between us that we dare not go any further down this particular lane of memories; it might be too sad and too nostalgic, and we're here to rekindle friendships for now and the future. Brady picks up the slack and engages Monica and Pierre in more conversation about their work at the school.

Toying with my salad, I can't help myself and recall good times with Betsy, Debbie, and Jenny, especially the Thanksgiving dinner they prepared for me, and that jar of cranberry jam. All those staff teas we went to at the school's boardinghouses. The times I thought I'd put my foot in my mouth, until Jenny admonished me, gently but firmly, not to get my "knickers in a twist." What is it about these people and their culture that makes me so happy, so at peace with life, even in the midst of the news of Jenny's death? I think it's about how the English live and the way they find something positive and humorous in all situations. Levity can be a wonderful anecdote when we receive bad news or feel sad; we must try to draw from the goodness of life in some way that reminds us of better times and the healing power of humor.

I'm gently reunited with my companions as Monica announces, "It's been lovely to see you both again after all these years. Since you're retired, you can come back any time of the year. Don't wait another twenty years! And now I must get on. I have a meeting at half three." Monica's upbeat tone reminds me of how well the English do "get on." We promise to stay in touch, then hug each other and go our separate ways.

I want to see the Dragon again, but school is in session, and I remember the rule that unexpected visitors, even old dragons, should wait until the school day is done before venturing onto the campus. Still, it can't hurt if we just walk by on our way to Summertown. Brady and I cross Banbury Road and amble down Bardwell Road toward the school. Gunga Din comes into view. We stand under an old oak in front of one of the boardinghouses, and I am transported right back to where and when I said goodbye to Jenny, Betsy, and Debbie in July 1999. So much has changed since that day: Jenny's death; former colleagues gone to other places and other lives; even the tin can structure where I taught has been transformed into a three-story glass building. Yet so much remains the same: the sound of loud, happy children playing in the schoolyard; teachers carrying stacks of books; the smell of the river that runs through campus. My thoughts turn to Jenny. I hear her laugh and see her gently take the hand of a rambunctious dragon and lead him with the rest of her class into her room. How very different and difficult it must be for Jenny's colleagues not to have her with them. Such a hard change for them. Looking across at the huge oak trees that line the campus, I pull myself together and reach for some Kleenex in my purse. Despite this bit of melancholy, a quiet peace that I don't entirely understand wafts over me. Perhaps it's due in part to all the time that has passed and the ways in which I've changed since my Dragon days.

I do one thing at a time now. If I'm making soup, I don't do anything else except make soup. I also make fewer and shorter lists, and I don't have to remind myself to wash my hair anymore. A significant step toward this "new me" has come through conversations with my spiritual director and my practice of silent prayer. I am learning to listen more and talk less to God. I hand over my perfectionism to God, acknowledging that I may never be rid of it, as that is not the point. I'll have to do this time and time again for the rest of my life, but I've accepted that. My love of the impeccable is as much a part of me as my little toe, and every minute of every day, I have the freedom to hand it over to God. Together, we are transforming me into someone who doesn't try to control situations or people, but who delights in making a pot of soup.

What a gift it is to be here in Oxford. Watching students and teachers do what they have always done, I understand how time has worked on me. Now, I see clearly what was invisible to me these past twenty years as I struggled to become the teacher I wished to be, a teacher like Miss Gluding. My year at the Dragon School was teaching me all along how to live in the here and now, not in the past or the future, but in the present. Indeed, the present is all we really have. We can worry about the future, we can be anxious about the past, but to be able to live in the present is a gift. We should honor it, for each day is a day that will never come again.

I feel Brady clasp my hand as he whispers, "Barb, let's walk up to Summertown."

As we leave the Dragon campus, I return his squeeze. We walk in silence for a bit, and then I tell him, "I'm glad you're here with me. It would have been harder to hear the news about Jenny without you by my side."

Brady slows down and says, "I didn't know Jenny like you did, but I remember her as a vibrant and funny woman the few times I saw her with her husband at school functions. And, of course, I remember all the times she was such a help to you."

I smile at his words as we cross from Charbury Road onto Belbroughton and head into Summertown. After walking a bit, I tell him, "I'm shocked she died so young; she probably wasn't even out of her fifties. And James, her husband, and their four daughters, especially Jill, their oldest daughter, whom I taught—how hard it will be for them without her."

"Barb, your empathy for Jenny's family is lovely. What about trying to reach out to them to share your condolences?"

"That's a wonderful idea. It will give me some closure, and I hope it'll be meaningful for them to hear from someone who was part of Jenny's life when she was healthy and vibrant. I'll email Monica; she'll know how to reach James. Thank you, lovey. You are a blessing."

Brady kisses my forehead softly. We take hands and walk into the shopping area of Summertown. We find Patisserie Café, our favorite place to get a cuppa, and take seats by the big, leaded front window that looks out on Banbury Road. The linoleum tables from 1999 are still here, though now they have charging stations attached to them and the newspapers are gone. But the menu is the same, thank goodness, because I have a hankering for a caramel slice: crumbly graham cracker crust, a layer of caramel, and milk chocolate topping. Deadly!

We order and look around to see two boys and three girls sitting at a large round table across from us. The kids are probably about twelve or thirteen years old. From the logo on their rucksacks, I know they're from Cherwell School, which I often passed on my walk to the Dragon when I lived here. Cherwell is a state school, what is called a public school in the United States. The five students drink tea and chat enthusiastically about Admiral Nelson and the Battle of Trafalgar for a project they're working on together. How funny! When I was at the Dragon, "projects" were foreign to my students. Indeed, I remember when Debbie told me how all schools in England at that time frowned on such collaborations. "Get them through the national curriculum" was their mantra in 1999.

A server delivers a pot of tea and two caramel slices to our table. As I pour the tea, Brady tilts his head in the direction of the students and asks, "Do they remind you of your Milton students?"

I smile and concur that they do. "It's something about their confidence, yet the way they also question and check and double-check their assumptions and ideas with each other. Milton kids do that with aplomb; it's part of their DNA."

I taught middle-school English and performing arts at Milton Academy from 2008 to 2015 before retiring. My time at this venerable New England boarding and day school reminded me in some ways of the Dragon: Each hosted a diverse population and attracted quirky kids and teachers. At both schools, I taught boys and girls whose parents worked in factories, as well as children of famous artists and politicians. My time at Milton was wonderful and also very difficult. It was wonderful because I ended my career on my best note. My encomium, written by kids and colleagues, was read to an audience of students, teachers, parents, administrators, and alumni on my last day. I'm most grateful to have been recognized as a "master teacher," a "writing teacher who writes," a "grammar guru," and a "teacher who listens and is unafraid of challenges."

But Milton was one tough place in my early years at the school. I struggled with the same issues of perfectionism that I'd worked so hard to address at NCDS and at Fessenden. Some parents told me I wasn't a "Milton teacher" because I demanded too much from the kids. Certain colleagues discounted my ideas and opinions. Students observed their behavior and followed suit. I felt alone and unwanted in my first couple of years there.

At some point when I felt like leaving the school, my husband reminded me of my experience at the Dragon, which until I got to Milton I thought was the hardest thing I'd ever done. But then Milton seemed most challenging. So I used what I learned that year away from home to address the perfectionism creeping back into my teaching. I knew that my old behavior wasn't in my best interest, so I watched for signs of it: correcting every mistake, instead of focusing on one or two; feeling agitated when things in the classroom didn't go the way I'd planned; trying to control a situation that didn't have an obvious outcome. By the grace of God, I was able to see what I was doing and change directions: I focused on the mistakes that would benefit my students most and let the others go. I gave them more autonomy in assignments. I didn't get my knickers in a twist if their results weren't what I would have done. Eventually I understood that the only way I could address my perfectionism was to get to know it. What tended to set it off? How constant was it? What was I really striving for, besides perfection? My familiarity with it helped me see that even in retirement, I am still a work in progress. And this is probably true for all of us. How much better off we would be if we could recognize, name, and own our "dragons," and at the same time give ourselves credit for being works in progress?

I gave everything I had to my Milton students, but I also stopped worrying about whether every child understood everything I taught. This unconventional approach helped me step away from the "lecture" mode I'd fallen into, and soon I was considered a "Milton teacher." I would have been happy to remain at the school for longer, but increased initiatives surrounding technology and multiculturalism, as well as yearly curriculum revisions, led to unreasonable administrative demands, more meetings, and much less teaching. Overnight, I'd been replaced by websites that had all the information my students needed; my passion, knowledge, and experience were obsolete; and the joy I'd felt for decades when my feet hit the floor every school-day morning was gone.

All the rapid and dramatic changes in Milton's programming created more stress than I could handle. I had a wake-up call in the winter of 2014. On my way home from a typical school day of teaching three morning classes in a row, attending an hour-long curriculum meeting, teaching two afternoon classes back-to-back, racing across campus to a faculty meeting, and supervising a rowdy eighth-grade study hall, I realized, while inhaling a sandwich, that my chest felt as if an elephant were standing on it. I could hardly breathe. It was only a panic attack, but the ER cardiologist told me to rest for the next five days and "let up on all the stress, as panic attacks can lead to other cardiac episodes."

The Cherwell kids' chatter returns me to my tea and caramel slice. The students pack up their rucksacks and meander out of the café, chatting enthusiastically about their sports at school and their weekend plans. Brady has paid our bill, so we leave the café and take the number 7 bus to Hernes Road, where we lived in 1998–'99.

Alighting from the bus, we walk down the street that winds past the nursing home to our old flat building, the Westgate. Standing on the pavement, I look at the windows of what was our flat on the ground floor of the three-story brick building. "Oh my gosh, Brady. Look! Those blue gingham curtains are still there!"

"So they are. I don't mind them now!" he says, squinting at them in the sunlight.

"Ha! You weren't so fond of them in 1999!" I joke, gently slapping his back.

"Well, we all change, don't we? Look how much you've changed since we were here." Brady grins.

"True!" I say. We stand for a bit, just looking at the flat. I wonder who lives here now. Is it another teacher? A family? A retired person? I glance up at what was Jacqui's flat and think about all our good times together: tea, museums, concerts, Evensong, suppers. We saw her each summer in the early years of the millennium, when we did those house exchanges, but she moved to Cornwall to be with her ailing brother in 2008. What a good and dear friend she was to us both.

On our ride back to the city center, we enjoy passing by all the landmarks we know so well and those few that are no more. Our go-to Thai place for takeaway is still there, but the Lemon Tree Restaurant, where we celebrated our birthdays, is gone.

As the bus edges closer to the city center, some teenage girls lope down the Banbury Road. I am immediately with them in spirit. How classically girl-like they are: When one struts, they all strut; then comes the giggling, the throwing back of heads, grasping of ponytails, whispering behind cupped hands. They remind me of my NCDS students.

I taught at NCDS for eight years, and my time there was one of tremendous growth and change. While the Dragon will always hold first place in my heart, NCDS follows closely behind, not just for its stimulating academic environment or its dedication to educating girls but because it was a safe place to talk openly about God. The conversations I had with students and colleagues there led Brady and me to find an Episcopal church in Boston that we could call home.

Leaving NCDS for Milton was one of the most difficult decisions of my career because I loved the girls, the material I taught, and the close relationships I enjoyed with colleagues. And, in my usual fashion, I didn't want to disappoint the school's ethos that "we are all family, and we stay together." After taking on the role of chair of the steering committee for the school's self-study from 2006 to 2008, I was asked to be on the recommendations committee in 2008–'09. Having to do that felt like the straw that broke the camel's back, but I knew I couldn't say no. As John Donovan reminded me when I taught at Fessenden, "Extra duties are part and parcel of any independent school."

Nonetheless, at NCDS I also realized my dream of teaching high-school English. I'd never been given this opportunity at other schools, as I didn't have a master's degree in English, but my department head believed in my ability. "I don't know of anyone who has been successful in getting seventh-grade girls to actually like reading *Oliver Twist*. I've no doubt you can design and teach a stimulating honors English seminar for tenth graders. Besides, the girls will know what they're getting with you as their teacher!"

We read Austen, Dickenson, Wollstonecraft, Shakespeare, and Turgenev, along with twentieth-century world literature by Desai, Naipaul, Walcott, and Tagore. We wrote all kinds of genres. A favorite assignment required students to create a fictional correspondence between poet Philip Larkin and Jane Austen, detailing their views on marriage. Our once-a-week, ninety-minute seminar was precious time for us to talk freely as women about what it was and is like to be female in Austen's time and in our own. Several girls wrote to me years after I left NCDS to express how much this class inspired them to become serious writers.

Despite my penchant for living in the present, I now allow myself, from time to time, to journey back to my years in the classroom. So many wonderful moments with kids, parents, and colleagues flow through me, yet, curiously, these memories include my faults and failures and what I learned about the necessity of forgiveness. I needed to forgive myself many times in my career, as many times as or more times than my students forgave me. Come to think of it, those kids I taught twenty years ago here in Oxford weren't the only dragons in my classroom—I could be quite draconian myself. But God has a way of balancing things out. Had I not had the good fortune to teach at Fessenden, I might never have recognized my own dragons, nor had the opportunity to go to Oxford and become that teacher I'd wanted to be ever since I was in first grade.

Acknowledgments

I've had this book in my head for many years, and there are many friends, family members, and former students and colleagues who've encouraged me along the way. While I thank them all, I am especially indebted to my writing teachers at the GrubStreet international writing school in Boston. Alysia Abbott and Mary Carroll Moore admonished me to do what the poet Major Jackson once said: "Go to the well each day, even if you think it's dry." Once I had a first draft, I turned to my other GrubStreet teacher, Nadine Kenney Johnstone, for some coaching. Our work together gave me the courage to write about my struggles with perfectionism. Without Nadine's devoted guidance and commitment to my story, I doubt I would have ventured any further than that first draft.

I am deeply grateful for the opportunity to publish my memoir with She Writes Press and to work with its team of inspiring, dedicated women. Brooke Warner, publisher; Shannon Green, project manager; Krissa Lagos, navigator of such things as tip sheets; and Caitlin Hamilton, my publicist, gave unstintingly of their time and advice, along with patience and humor, to this often anxious author. This memoir would not have come to pass without the stellar guidance and care given to me by my editor, Annie Tucker. I am grateful beyond words for her encouragement and faith in me and my story.

Her eye for detail and her humor and friendship made the task of revision a pleasure; not to mention our mutual delight when we discovered we had Milton Academy in common, I as a teacher and she as a student, though, to my loss, not one of mine. What a joy it is to be her student and friend.

Several of my own schoolteachers are also to be acknowledged. Though most of them are no longer this side of heaven, I sense their presence with me when I write, as I often did when I was teaching. Miss Gray, Mrs. Berg, Mrs. Church, three English teachers extraordinaire, gave me a deep and abiding love for the English language, all the while demanding excellence from me. My thanks is paltry, but I trust they each know what they have meant and always will mean to me.

I wish to express my gratitude to the following schools where I taught from 1993 to 2015: the Fessenden School, the Dragon School, Newton Country Day School of the Sacred Heart, and Milton Academy. My years at each of these institutions were challenging and fruitful, and I am deeply grateful for the many friendships formed and the life-changing experiences afforded me in their halls of learning.

And then there are my students. I probably taught more than 1,500 kids between 1980 and 2015. To all of them, I am indebted. Indebted for putting up with my perfectionism, tolerating my mistakes, going along with my antics in class, and suffering through "too much grammar." The best part about being a teacher is the opportunity to know many of my students as they are now, young women and men who are thriving and who, if they remember me as being a "really hard teacher," do so with affection and humor. To all of them, I express my love and gratitude for their friendship and for the good and the hard times we shared so many years ago.

Finally, and certainly not least, I thank my long-suffering husband, Brady Millican. He lovingly tolerated my five hour writing streaks, the papering of our dining room with giant Post-it notes, and expletives from my third-floor study whenever the manuscript temporarily disappeared into cyberspace, yet he was always there with a cup of tea, a glass of wine, dinner made. His forbearance and stellar proofreading are miles beyond what is reasonable to expect. It is to him that, with all my love, I dedicate my first book.

Nota bene: All the names of the people with whom I worked—students, parents, teachers, and administrators—have been changed to protect their privacy.

About the Author

© Dream Media LLC

Barbara Kennard was born and raised in Montclair, New Jersey. She holds an AMI degree (Association Montessori International) from the Montessori Center of New Jersey, where she trained with one of Maria Montessori's students, and a double master's degree in special education and clinical child development from Pacific Oaks College. She completed her undergraduate work and California Teaching Certification at Occidental College. Barbara taught English and performing arts to elementary-, middle-, and high-school students from 1980 to 2015 in a variety of settings: public, private, non-sectarian, sectarian, special needs, suburban, rural, and inner-city. She has received two teaching awards: the Christa McAuliffe Award for Teaching Excellence and the Barbara Kennard Sixth Grade

English Prize, established in her name at the Fessenden School by a Fessenden family. Her poetry has been published in the United States and in the United Kingdom in the *Anglican Theological Review*, *Boomerang: A UK Online Poetry Journal*, *Time of Singing*, the *New Writer*, and *Teachers' Forum*, a Milton Academy publication. Barbara is a member of the Fellowship of St. John, a community of lay women and men around the world who strive to live the Rule of Life followed by the Brothers of the Society of St. John the Evangelist in Cambridge, Massachusetts. Barbara enjoys gardening, swimming, reading theology, cooking, and volunteering for her church's mission and outreach programs. She has lived in California, New York, New Jersey, Massachusetts, and Oxford, England, but now resides in Texas with her husband, pianist Brady Millican, and their cat, Piper.

SELECTED TITLES FROM SHE WRITES PRESS

She Writes Press is an independent publishing company founded to serve women writers everywhere. Visit us at www.shewritespress.com.

What They Didn't Burn: Uncovering My Father's Holocaust Secrets, Mel Laytner $16.95, 9781684631032
What if you uncovered a cache of buried Nazi documents that revealed your father as a man very different than the one you knew—or thought you knew? In this poignant memoir, Mel Laytner, a former reporter, peels away layers of his father's stories to expose painful truths about surviving the Holocaust and its aftermath.

The Restless Hungarian: Modernism, Madness, and The American Dream, Tom Weidlinger $16.95, 978-1-943006-96-0
A revolutionary, a genius, and a haunted man . . . The story of the architect-engineer Paul Weidlinger, whose colleagues called him "The Wizard," spans the rise of modern architecture, the Holocaust, and the Cold War. The revelation of hidden Jewish identity propels the author to trace his father's life and adventures across three continents.

Engineering a Life: A Memoir, Krishan K. Bedi $16.95, 978-1-943006-43-4
A memoir of Krishan Bedi's experiences as a young Indian man in the South in the 1960s, this is a story of one man's perseverance and determination to create the life he'd always dreamed for himself and his family, despite his options seeming anything but limitless.

Social Media Isn't Social: Rediscovering the lost art of face-to-face communication, Al Maag $15, 978-1940716459
With humor and insight born of decades of experience, Al Maag shares what he learned during his Chicago childhood in the 1950s and 60s, a stark contrast to the current C-generation that has grown up with electronic gadgets. *Social Media Isn't Social* shows why online social media cannot replace face-to-face human connection, and reveals the critical real-life social skills you need to succeed today in business and in life.